The CB Cowboys
The Saga of the Legendary Christensen Family

Billy Wilcoxson

EAKIN PRESS Fort Worth, Texas
www.EakinPress.com

Copyright © 2003
By Vicki Christensen Felder
Published By Eakin Press
An Imprint of Wild Horse Media Group
P.O. Box 331779
Fort Worth, Texas 76163
1-817-344-7036
www.EakinPress.com
ALL RIGHTS RESERVED
1 2 3 4 5 6 7 8 9
ISBN-10: 1-57168-823-4
ISBN-13: 978-1-57168-823-1
Library of Congress Control Number 2003115842

In memory of Henry Christensen, Bill Markley, Ben Johnson, Reg Kesler, Bob Cook, Warren Siegal, and all the other twisters who have taken the last trail home.

Contents

Preface vii
Introduction ix

Part One / The Early Years
1. The Foundation 3
2. The Jaws of a Cougar 14
3. Spencer Butte 19
4. Edgar Buchanan and His Traveling Trio 25
5. The Three Sisters 29
6. The Origin of the Christensen Brothers Rodeo 40
7. Romance on the Camas Swale 47
8. The Fourth of July 1929 50

Part Two / The CB Cowboys
9. Lost at Sea 59
10. The Girl from Alberta 63
11. Wimpy the Sheep Dog 66
12. The Pony Express 72
13. Lynx Hollow 74
14. One Life Taken, One Life Given 79
15. Miss Klamath's Last Jump 83
16. Snowman and Iceman 87
17. Two for One 91
18. The Calgary Stampede 95
19. The First NFR 99

20.	The Happy Valley Ranch	103
21.	Ridin' Ol' Paint	107
22.	Crash and Burn	113
23.	The Blizzard of '69	116
24.	The Higgley Hop	121
25.	St. Paul and Molalla	126
26.	Other Great Christensen Brothers Broncs	132
27.	The Right Doctor Might Have Saved Her	137
28.	Hawk Eye, Bull, Droopy and Hooter	140
29.	The Lovely Trick-Riding Christensen Girls	142

Part Three / On Top of the World

30.	On Down the Road	151
31.	The Hot Red Fire Engine	156
32.	The Pendleton Roundup	159
33.	The Cow Palace	162
34.	The Diamond Horseshoe	169
35.	The Beginning of the End	173
36.	The Fall of the Christensen Empire	177

Epilogue	185
Glossary	187
Appendix	
I. Christensen Brothers NFR Stock	189
II. Famous Christensen Brothers Saddle Broncs	195
III. Famous Christensen Brothers Bulls	197

Preface

As a small child growing up on the family ranch in the lush valleys of western Oregon, I had no idea that a book about my family would ever be written. I realize now that there is a story to be told. Not one of make-believe, for if it was, much would be changed. Instead, it's a story of real life, filled with triumph and tragedy, of laughter and tears. A story of a family living and working together to build what others only dream about.

From the banks of the Allegheny River in 1864 to the dusty rodeo arenas scattered throughout the Pacific Northwest, the story spans four generations and recounts a time in America when old met new. My grandmother, Mollie Christensen, was born in the back of a covered wagon and lived to see men walk on the moon. At no other time in history would this be possible.

Growing up, life was centered around the ranch. The outside world seemed far away. The price of cattle, the weather, and how many head of bucking stock would be needed for the next rodeo were the main topics of conversation. When the dinner bell rang, all who heard were welcome to sit at Grandma's table.

Sadly, this family, once very close, was forced to walk away from all that was familiar. One day, when a sheriff's auction had been scheduled after we had exhausted all avenues to sell the ranches, Grandma, who was ninety-two, looked me straight in the eyes and said, "Well, at least we did it. Lots of folks never have the opportunity."

Looking back, I know that no matter where life takes us, we

will always be together, if in memory only: sitting in Grandma's kitchen with her cookstove burning warmly, discussing the day's events and planning tomorrows.

This family history consists of the recollections of my father, Bob Christensen, and other family members, as told to the author, Billy Wilcoxson. Events and conversations are detailed as accurately as possible, based on the memories of those who shared their stories. Photographs which do not list a credit are from the family's collection. Due to the number of photos and span of coverage, it was not possible to verify the source for some; however, every effort was made to properly identify and credit them.

—Vicki Christensen Felder

Introduction

In this book, written in three parts, you will escape the humdrum life of today. You will walk and gallop and laugh and cry and love and live through the evolution of an empathetic, passionate, courageous, and famous American family.

In the beginning you will become acquainted with two newlywed Bohemian kids who immigrated to America in 1864, and you'll ride with them over trails in a wagon train pioneering west.

The value of their lineage will be ascertained by the actions of one of their offspring, who with her husband and descendants established and operated one of the largest cattle and sheep ranches in Oregon. They would become one of the most celebrated stock contracting companies in the history of rodeo: the "Christensen Brothers Rodeo Company."

When the Christensen Brothers put their first rodeo outfit together in 1929, the trails of rodeo were still being blazed, even though it had been around for over seventy years. Until only recently, the general public looked upon rodeo as a Wild West show or circus. They failed to see cowboys as athletes; rather, they saw red-necked, illiterate, hayseed hoodlums who only came to town to get drunk. They had no idea that many cowboys were, and still are, college-educated, staunch family men and Christians, as well as some of the most supreme and courageous athletes in the history of the world.

It's my belief that the general public has blinders on. Little do they know that cowboys are, and always have been, nonconformists among an imprisoned civilization—a civilization locked within the prison of a skeptical, wishy-washy society, wandering aimlessly through the hypocrisy of a plastic, smoggy, modern existence. The freedom and spirit of the cowboy have always been the envy of the outside world.

Many of our ancestors gave birth to the sport of rodeo: the old-timey bronco-riding, steer-roping, hardy cowpunchers of the Old West; the lean, tan-faced, bold young knights of the saddle.

In a time when thousands of herds were driven across the vast and windy Texas plains to the railheads in Kansas and prairies north, these hard-twisted cowpunchers left their brand and scattered their salt on the history of America. For fifty or so years the never-ending red winds of Texas and Oklahoma rolled restless tumbleweeds over the old hoof-worn trails to Kansas and north to Montana.

Then came the rushing new society of the twentieth century, replacing the cattle trails with asphalt highways. But the cowboy endured, evolving into the resilient young contestants of today.

Since the fall of the historic Christensen Brothers, that legendary Oregon ranch family, many have been interested in their story. Such interest seved as the roots of this book.

In an interview with Troy Schwindt, staff writer for the *Las Vegas Sun,* legendary and outstanding six-time World Champion All-Around Larry Mahan had this to say:

"I spent a lot of time with the Christensen Brothers while I was growing up. They were instrumental in my whole deal. I won my first bull riding title at a Christensen Brothers rodeo in Klamath Falls, Oregon, in 1960. That was a big deal. The brothers provided me with stock to practice on, and that was a wonderful experience. They enjoyed their rodeo life and they had fun. It was just a hell of an experience."

If the Christensen Brothers had ever gotten back all the money they loaned to cowboys for entry fees, they each would have been millionaires twice over.

Cowboys loved them, and they loved cowboys.

After hanging up my spurs and taking up the pen, I often imagined what a privilege it would be to write the epic of this renowned rodeo outfit. Then, by a stroke of fate's hand, that became possible.

During the NFR in Las Vegas, Nevada, I was at the Gold Coast Hotel and Casino watching the rodeo on big-screen TV in one of the showrooms. The big room was packed. Finding a seat was comparable to getting one at the live performance in the Thomas and Mack Center. As I looked around the room for a chair, I noticed an extra one at Vicki and Eddie Felder's table and boldly walked over to ask if they could spare the room for my company. They welcomed me wholeheartedly. I pulled out a chair and sat down.

I didn't really know the Felders, but I had seen Vicki, Bobby Christensen's lovely daughter, when she was a trick rider. It was apparent the Christensen genealogy enhanced her looks.

Along about the time of the calf roping, they asked if I might be interested in writing this story.

I was overwhelmed, feeling like the luckiest man alive to be presented with the honor.

When I was a button in my teens and had chosen to make my mark as a bronc rider, I saved up a few bucks, bought an old junker, loaded the trunk, and headed out. I had no idea that bucking horses could be as outstanding as the ones Bobby, Jr. and Hank Christensen hauled. Then I went to one of their rodeos and found the meaning in the saying: "There are bucking horses and there are BUCKING horses!"

On the rodeo trail for fifteen years, I never stepped across the chute to get on a bronc that was any better than a Christensen Brothers horse. There have never been bucking horses more outstanding or remarkable than ponies like Miss Klamath and War Paint. Both bucked off some of the greatest bronc riders who have ever lived. To name a few, Casey Tibbs, Bill Linderman, Deb Copenhaver, Shawn Davis, Larry Mahan, Phil Lynn, Marty Wood, and Winston Bruce—all past champions.

I'm not one to procrastinate and wasn't about to wait for the grass to grow under my feet, so a few days after the Finals I packed for a trip to Aztec, New Mexico. When I rolled in, I found Eddie and Vicki at their trophy buckle manufacturing company, Frontier Trophy Buckles, where we had a little meeting dealing with the details of this writing project. Within a few days I began to write the most dynamic story of my career.

* * *

The mid-December morning was brisk as he followed a welcome smile out on the porch of his little house to greet me in his shirtsleeves and slippers. His small, alert eyes were filled with wisdom. His shirt and jeans were pressed, his hair combed. We shook hands, and he invited me in.

When you walk into an old bronc rider's camp, it's no surprise to see a muddle of dusty remnants and smell the stench of stale air. It's to be expected when there's no woman around to pick things up and knock off the dust.

At eighty-seven most old-timers are so crippled up they can hardly gimp across the kitchen floor to run down their pill bottles. In the search they're usually either grumbling about losing their glasses or growling about the shape of the weather. Most of the time they forget what they're looking for. If you have a pertinent issue of business to be discussed and can pry them into a conversation on the matter, it's likely, after a few sentences, they will drift into reminiscence of some old story irrelevant to the subject at hand. You can barely stay abreast of the words rolling over their smooth gums and wrinkled lips.

Not so in the case of Albert Bobby Christensen, the only brother left alive from one of the greatest stock contracting outfits in the history of rodeo. His whetted words were as clear as those of a twenty-year-old, but he had a sort of lonesomeness in his tone. And I could tell he was tied hard and fast to the memories of his glory days. Yet he didn't dwell on the glitter and glamour he had lived in rodeo arenas for fifty years. I suppose being in the spotlight had never mattered much to him.

Have you ever heard a melody in the wind as you followed a cow to the home ranch under the light of the Milky Way, or fanned a bad one with your hat, or ridden along a lonesome ridge tracking a cougar or a big buck? Those are the memories I heard in his voice and saw in his eyes.

His humble home was clean and bright. A few rodeo pictures and a game trap he had invented, mounted on a golden plaque, were hanging on the walls, as were the heads of a big black bear, a red bear, and two coyotes.

The flames dancing through the glass doors of a little wood-burning stove were flickering cozily and summoning me with welcoming warmth. The smell of strong coffee, drifting from the small tidy kitchen, calmed the mood for the powwow about to take place. The coffee filled the morning with an aroma to welcome weary travelers or wandering cowhands.

Bobby poured us a cup and sat down across from me in his easy chair. I turned on my tape recorder, and he began telling the story you are about to read.

After reviewing the tape, I began writing the story in my own words. Having been raised on a cattle ranch, by old-time cowboys, I picked up on the unusual dialogue and mannerisms.

I had never dreamed of becoming a writer. Being a cowboy was all I thought of. I had begun rodeoing at an early age and stayed on the rodeo trail until I started writing my first book, *Ten Karat Hole in a Donut*. With my knowledge of rodeo and the ways of the old-timers who raised me, looking at a cow's rear end, I have penned this book in true authenticity.

As told to me.

—BILLY WILCOXSON

Part One

The Early Years

1

The Foundation

Only a handful of settlers had reached the Oregon Territory before the Gold Rush of '49. When wind of the great gold strike blew across the country, thousands of hardy souls pointed their eyes, spread their wings, and fled west, hoping to gorge their glut of wealth from the rugged mountains and unexplored streams of California.

Too late to get rich with gold, and long before Bohemia became Czechoslovakia, a young man named Michael Almasie and his fourteen-year-old bride, Christina, whom he preferred to call Suzy, sailed to America in 1863.

It was raining when they arrived, but they hardly noticed. Little was on their minds except securing shelter and employment.

The big steamer's baritone horn announced its arrival when it docked at Hudson Bay. The two young immigrants hurried down the congested gangplank, thriving with excitement, swirling in the flood of other hopefuls.

With only a few dollars and the same dreams that millions of other poorly educated immigrants had come to find in America, Michael and Suzy were content to face the hardships that lie ahead. Surely there would be work in a city the size of New York, here in this wonderful new country.

Suzy could scarcely keep up with her husband's long stride as they followed the crowd through the overcrowded, muddy street. Construction was booming. Buildings were going up in every block. New streets were being built and old ones resurfaced. Men of every color, race, and creed labored everywhere, and big, bold horses shouldered their strength against heavy lumber wagons sunk to the hubs in boggy ruts.

Michael had heard that big money was being made building homes in Million-Dollar Row, up on Knob Hill. After finding a room in a ramshackle hotel and getting a good night's sleep, he left Suzy with a little money to shop for groceries from vendors along Broadway and struck out for Million-Dollar Row.

Suzy had cooked on a friendly Bohemian woman's fire behind the hotel and had supper ready for Michael when he got home late that evening. He wasn't hungry; he had found no job.

But there was talk of work in the coal mines, so the robust young man and his wife made their way to Pennsylvania. Michael found work in the mines.

While her husband worked, Suzy was left to fight a war with layers of dust that had found serenity in the stillness of the one-room shack long before they rented it. The dust had blown through the cracks for months and vigorously rejected her efforts to send it packing, but it was no match against her swift, strong arms. The sulking black widows sensed the danger when she went for the corners. They clung to their webs while she whacked her broom against the gray, un-planed board walls. The thick brown water she wrung from her heavy mop proved to be another resisting opponent. Trying to escape the calamity invading their abode, friendly long-legged granddaddy spiders would flee for refuge as swiftly as their lanky, stilt-like legs could carry their tiny bodies.

To Suzy, the only difference between her home job and Michael's in his hellhole was the danger lurking at his. She had revealed her anxiety to him about the risky work when he found the job, and relayed horrifying tales she had heard about frequent visits from the "Grim Reaper"—how he'd creep from the darkness wearing his black-hooded robe and wielding his razory scythe on his mission to snuff the flame from hat lanterns with his long, ugly fingers and smother any further life from the trapped miners with tons of falling earth. Stories abounded about the unstable cribbing in the tunnels hundreds of feet below the surface. Cave-ins were common.

But, as time would tell, Suzy had married a solid, hard-working, and fearless young man. Her worries went unheeded, and she soon learned to respect his decisions.

Barely fifteen, Suzy experienced her first painful joy in having a baby. Anna was born in the spring of 1864. A year later, Beth was born. It was plain to see that the family needed more room.

Michael located an old four-bedroom, two-story house in Allegheny County, a few miles north of Pittsburgh. Suzy was skeptical when Michael told her he was tired of renting and wanted to buy the old house. The asking price of $2,000 was an amount neither had ever seen.

It was a fifty-mile drive for them to look at the house. The owner was a broad-shouldered, square-jawed old gentleman, with the battles he had won far behind him. He drove the couple in his beautiful carriage. Suzy had never ridden in a carriage.

A decrepit picket fence separated the long-neglected yard from a rough, seldom-used road. The arms of sappy ancient elms were bountiful with shade for both sides of the road. A traditional gazebo, many years past its prime, stood ten yards from the house, grieving for the laughter of children; it yielded to her the sounds of "Ring around the Roses" once more.

Spring showers had kept the yard green with tall grass and thriving weeds. A loaded trellis flourishing with red and pink roses allowed only a few beams of afternoon sunlight to peek inside the weathered front porch.

The screen door squeaked when the old man pulled it open. Michael and Suzy stood behind him while he fumbled with a skeleton key to unlock the front door.

Coal-burning stoves claimed legroom in both the huge front room and kitchen. There were two downstairs bedrooms and two upstairs. From an upstairs window, Michael could see the privy, its door in need of hinge work.

Suzy saw possibilities in the once beautiful, time-worn estate, but she couldn't fathom the idea of them being able to buy it. Two thousand dollars was an extreme barrier.

When Michael handed the owner the $30 down payment (a month's wages for his foreman's status), Suzy's worrying nature automatically sent a message of panic to her brain. But there was no room for debate with Michael. She knew she would hit a brick wall if she expressed even a fraction of opposition related to the matter. After nine years, first as his sweetheart since she was six, then as his wife for three years, and having endured the insurmountable hardships that accompany the first years of marriage, she knew him very well.

They agreed to pay $30 a month for ten years with $1,070 in interest.

A hammer, a saw, and a mouthful of nails were Michael's companions for the first two years they lived there. When he wasn't in the dungeon, he built most of the furniture for the house.

Suzy also had an overwhelming amount of energy and put her creative arranging and decorating touches to work, resurrecting every room from the dead and keeping them spotless. She repaired and painted the fence, the gazebo, and the privy, and as if that wasn't enough, she built a milking shed.

Defying pain in the form of daily bouts of depression, as she was pregnant with her third child, she met her husband's needs and breast-fed and mothered two rambunctious children. She also cut firewood, cooked three hot meals on a wood stove daily, fed and milked the cow, churned butter, made cottage cheese, swept, dusted, scrubbed on her knees, scrubbed on her washboard, and made and mended clothes. She weeded and irrigated a garden, tended the yard, fought mosquitoes and summer sunburns, and shoveled the footpath to the mailbox routinely in the winter.

Joe was their third child, followed by Andy and then Michael, Jr.

As the years left wrinkled and callused hands on Michael and Suzy, the children grew, and Michael's pioneering spirit began to gnaw at the marrow of his soul.

Suzy had been expecting another child for nearly four months when the news of a wagon train, soon to be rolling through Pennsylvania, reached them. Michael drew his family together in the big front room of their home and told them he would soon tip his hat to the boardwalks in Oregon.

After detailed planning for the trip and penciling their budget, Michael bought supplies along with four head of Clydesdales and a massive prairie schooner in preparation of joining the other pioneers in the long trek.

Joe was now a strapping twenty-year-old. Andy was nineteen. They helped Michael load the schooner. When stacking the furniture, they left room for a pallet to make the trip as comfortable for Suzy as they could.

The day the long-expected wagon train heading for California, Oregon, and points north came in view, the whole Almasie family watched from their front porch. An untallied conglomeration of barking mongrels was trotting alongside the train. People were riding horses or mules; several were walking. A number of milk cows and bawling calves were tied behind some of the wagons.

Michael crafted his team into position behind the last wagon in the train. Everyone was filled with optimistic excitement, especially he and the children.

The wagon master, a tall, tan frontiersman dressed in buckskin, called back to the drivers: "Roll 'em!"

Echoing commands of drivers and a rhapsody of cracking whips mingling through the air awakened the burdened horses and lethargic oxen teams.

"Haw! Get up there!"

"Haw! Get in that harness, Buck!"

"Haw! Get up!"

Harnessed brutes challenged the weight of the heavy wagons.

Trace chains rattled and clanged. Tugs stretched and squeaked, and creaking wheels began rolling.

With Suzy beside him on the high seat, Michael shook his lines. His bullwhip uncoiled and cracked like a pistol shot over the wheelers. "Haw!" The four big horses drove their bulging shoulders into the harness and followed the train snaking out behind the tall frontiersman.

Suzy's eyes clouded when she looked back to see her old dreams and friends blend with the dust and fade into oblivion.

Theirs was only one of hundreds of wagon trains that had headed west following the end of the bloodiest war in the history of America. Train after long train of covered wagons, loaded to the axles with household goods, family heirlooms, and delicate furniture, staged a monumental exodus west.

Moving perilously in ruts made by earlier pioneers on a dim trail out of Pennsylvania, the Almasie wagon bobbed and weaved awkwardly with the long white train. After two days and one night they reached the east bank of the massive, untamed Allegheny. Heavy rain clouds drifted in, hiding the moon and stars before they camped. It was all but impossible to remove harness and yoke from the animals until the cooking fires lit the darkness.

By morning the storm clouds had drifted west.

The midday sun found the men busy loading livestock on three huge barges capable of transporting thirty to forty tons apiece.

Suzy, little Mike, and the girls were perched on the schooner watching a side-wheel steamboat paddling lethargically down the Allegheny. Neighborly foghorns bellowed a greeting to the dismembered wagon train. Glamorous ladies, dressed in high-fashion styles only old money from Million-Dollar Row could buy, lent charm to the long, glistening oak deck of the grand floating castle. The beautiful women strolled leisurely under vogue Panama hats, twisting pink and yellow parasols over their shoulders, and arm in arm with handsome gentlemen, outfitted in top hat and tails.

Even after twenty years in America, Suzy and Michael's English was still harnessed with a Bohemian lilt. Each of their American-born children had only a slight eastern accent.

"Do you think there are steamboats in Oregon, Mama?" Anna asked.

Suzy's hands were folded over the child inside her. She shrugged in response to Anna.

Beth, with Mike in her lap, had blossomed into a pretty young lady of twenty.

She looked away from the paddlewheel and picked out a meandering cloud. "Aren't they beautiful, Mother?"

Suzy nodded and stroked Mike's cowlick.

By the time the train was across the river and ready to roll, Andy took the driving lines from his father's hands and told him to rest. They camped near Moon Run that night.

As the days crept by, the hems of the girls' dresses began to wear from dragging on the ground, and the sun began to fade their bonnets. They longed to shake out their hair and throw away their old, badly scuffed clodhoppers and slip on their soft, high-button calfskin shoes.

As they followed the wagon into a gully, Anna tripped and fell down the bank. Beth helped her to her feet and hurried to keep up with the wagon. Anna, feeling a sting in her knees, lifted her dress to find one knee skinned and the other only red. She licked her palm and cooled her wounds, then trotted to catch the wagon.

When passing through Illinois, the girls constantly fought the wind to keep it from snatching the skirts of their dresses and lifting them above their knees.

The wind strengthened even more after they left Illinois. Hostile lightning began to light the Iowa sky. Thunder began to rumble behind the churning clouds. Michael stopped the wagon and yelled for Beth and Anna to get in with Suzy and Mike. The wind became savage, lashing the schooners and threatening to rip their canvas tops to shreds. Blinding in her fury, Mother Nature emptied her bowels over the country for miles around, and inside of thirty minutes the storm seized the train and locked it in mud.

As fierce lightning lit the sky amid waves of clapping thunder, panic struck. The perplexed horses and rebelling oxen chose to disobey the cracking bullwhips. The wagon master spurred his horse every jump. His strong hindquarters and powerful gaskin muscles propelled the horse through the boggy muck from one wagon to the next.

"Keep 'em movin'!" the Texan shouted.

Andy, Joe, Beth, and Anna were pushing their wagon. Even though Mike was only five, he was trying to help. Michael stood to control his confused, squealing horses. The two leaders went straight up, pawing at the blinding rain, and puffs of smoke dried the mud wherever lightning struck. The sky continued to roar. It seemed as though the whole world would shake apart.

In moments that seemed like an eternity, Michael managed to get the team lined out, and the heavy wagon slowly began to budge. The children were gasping with exhaustion when they felt the wagon move without their help. Joe lifted Mike over the tailgate to stay inside with Suzy.

Desperate voices were screaming from every direction, and youngsters cried in terror. Wagons were stuck everywhere.

A nearby woman's scream shrieked through the mayhem. Her feminine voice was certainly no match with the wild panic, refusing to calm.

Andy snapped his eyes toward the scream. The driving rain was hampering his sight. He wiped them with his shirtsleeve until he could see Margaret Massengale, a young widow. Her two-horse team was dragging her beside her small wagon. Andy floundered toward her, gaining momentum until he reached her and dragged her to her feet. He grabbed the driving lines from her hands.

The fear-stricken team was lunging ahead four feet at a time. They jerked Andy down. He struggled until he had his balance and legs again, then pulled and heaved until he finally stopped the horses. Climbing up on the wagon seat, he stomped the foot brake and wrapped the lines around it.

Beth heard him yell for her to attend to Margaret, and she ran to comfort Margaret and help her back on her wagon after Andy was off.

The Almasie wagon was stuck once more. Andy and Beth sloshed toward the wagon to help Joe and Anna push. Thunder exploded. Lightning burst through the sky and struck near Michael's horses. They tilted the wagon on two wheels when the rearing leaders jumped sideways, and two wheels sank in the mud. The horses continued to fight.

Suddenly Anna slipped and fell under a back wheel. It took every fiber in Michael's body to hold the four horses until Beth and Joe pulled Anna to safety.

The horses lunged, jerking the wagon out of the bog. It dropped to its belly and jerked the horses to an abrupt stop.

The storm stopped as suddenly as it had started. The thunder hushed. The lightning spent its anger and gave the sky a lovely rainbow. Every person and animal in the train had fought ferociously to beat nature's scorn, and they had won!

After leaving two months behind, they connected to the Oregon Trail in western Nebraska. By the time they saw the Snake River in Idaho, the adventure had lasted nearly five months, spanning close to 3,000 miles through seven states.

Everything in the day was beautiful when the wagon master halted the train and aired a message. Those near enough to hear him were told to be extra careful when crossing the river. The crossing was shallow and bulging with boulders beneath the waves, many the size of watermelons.

Michael lifted his hat and sat it between himself and Joe. He wiped his brow with his shirtsleeve and spoke down to Beth and Anna, who were standing beside the front wagon wheel.

"How is your mother doing now, Beth?"

The family was concerned about Suzy, as she neared the birthing time of her sixth child.

"She's resting well, Poppa," Beth replied.

"Good," Michael said. "Go to the wagon of Mr. Brooks. Tell Andrew he must come to our wagon. He needs to help his brother cross the river. I will be with your mother at that time."

Beth hurried past the three wagons in front of them and stopped near the wheel on the passenger's side at the next. She greeted Mr. Brooks and relayed Michael's message to Andy.

Taking the lines from his father, who crawled into the back with Suzy, Joe drove the horses ahead as the train crawled across the Snake. When he reached the river he curled his hands, pulling the lines to check the leaders. The wheelers were well broke and checked themselves to keep from crowding the leaders. It was as though they had magic in their feet, the way they controlled their bodies, carefully feeling their way off the steep bank and into the rapid water.

Moving northwest after the train crossed the Snake, most of the folks would settle in or near Pendleton at the end of the Oregon Trail.

The Almasies split off when they reached the John Day River in Oregon, continuing due west with thirty or so other wagons. The family rolled along the John Day for four days, camping on her banks.

Suzy's labor began before sundown. She could deliver at any time.

While the others were sitting by a small fire, fishing that night, she lay under a quilt she had made. She patted her tummy and began to think about the trip she had just made in her condition. Suzy was proud of her little family. They had stumbled blindly through dust storms, forged raging rivers, ridden until they were stiff, walked until they gave out, sweated until they fell. Defeated three violent storms, conquered scores of steep mountains and jagged canyons, battled blood-sucking mosquitoes and ticks, outwitted water moccasins and rattlers. And through it all they had watched over her intensely. They had sung to her, prayed with her, wept with her, laughed with her, and changed strangers into loving friends.

Beth and Anna were sitting on the ground, leaning against

one of the wagon's rear wheels, talking, when Suzy's water broke. She calmly called for Beth.

Beth sent Anna running to bring a midwife who had been looking in on Suzy regularly. As she dashed toward the midwife's wagon, Anna called out to Michael and the boys. Michael held a lantern and told Anna and the boys they didn't have any business being present during the birthing procedure.

Beth, however, helped the midwife, and a beautiful baby girl was born within an hour.

Mollie Mary Almasie would grow into a unique, strong-willed woman someday. Her genes would be passed down to a generation of one of the most well-known, loved and respected offspring who ever burned their brand in Oregon.

2

The Jaws of a Cougar

The Almasies' homestead was located at Lake Creek, a tiny town between the tiny settlement of Mapleton and Florence, a prospering logging camp. Lake Creek itself ran a strong head of water, fed by mountain streams the year round, and spilled into Triangle Lake, near Mapleton.

Timber, Oregon's most precious commodity, was so thick it was blinding. Logging companies were skimming their payrolls from the soaring pine forests all over the Northwest.

Mapleton was a one-horse town with only a few log cabins, a barbershop, a mercantile store, a saloon, a post office, and a train station, where the tracks looped and headed back to Eugene, the logging trains' point of departure. The narrow, single-gauge track was a spur off the mainline that skirted along several logging camps. About once a month the lonesome little tumbleweed burg of Mapleton came alive when folks came to town for supplies. The storekeeper and barkeep rolled out the red carpet. The barber raised the price for a haircut from a dime to fifteen cents. Anyone who needed to make a train trip boarded in Mapleton.

Some of the camps were equipped with small but efficient mills. There were no such things as chainsaws in those days.

Timber was harvested with twenty-foot manual crosscut. The days were long, and the work was tough.

After the lumberjacks had a day's worth of trees down and the grunts had them limbed, the muleskinners skidded the logs to the mills, where buzz saws would turn raw timber into boards. The wild game must have been puzzled with the noise from the idling steam engines, the little puffing gray clouds chugging from them as the men loaded the lumber onto the flatcars. The logging train would haul the cargo to Eugene to connect with the main line, and the lumber was shipped nationwide.

To estimate how much timber was logged in those mountains would only be a wild guess.

In 1909, when the Almasies' youngest child, Mollie, was sixteen, she went to work cooking for twenty men in the logging camp at Florence. She was a pretty young lady, slim and fairly tall, with her mother's good looks and her father's coal black hair. All the loggers took a shine to her. She had no interest in any of them.

Then one day, when she was eighteen, a young logger in his early twenties named Lawrence Christensen came to work at Florence.

He resembled Mollie's father in many ways: a solid frame, blue eyes, good manners, a pleasant nature and sense of humor, as well as stamina. Equally important to a young lady, he was easy to look at, and he caught Mollie's eye right off.

Born in Denver, Lawrence grew up logging, mostly in Colorado, Wyoming, Montana, and Idaho. Before he came to work at Florence, he had been logging the Snake River country of Idaho.

After putting in his first day at Florence, Lawrence stood in line with the crew to wash up for supper. The delicious aroma of chicken frying was drifting out of the cookshack. After the lumberjack ahead of him threw his dirty wash water out of the tin wash pan and dried his hands and face on one of five towels hanging on nails driven into the trunk of a big pine, Lawrence took off his hat and pitched it under the tree. His white forehead contrasted with his sun-browned face. He scrubbed his hands and face and moved out of the way for the next man.

Lawrence's uncombed hair was thick. He smoothed it back with his callused fingers and headed for the tent.

It was hard for him not to notice Mollie when he walked inside the big tent. She was at the wood cookstove frying chicken with her back to him. Although the washing line outside had dwindled down to only two men, there was still plenty of room on the wooden benches at the long table for him to sit down. He found room in front of a tin plate and an empty cup. He could hardly keep his eyes off her as she moved across the floor with both hands full and placed a platter of biscuits in front of him and a big bowl of black-eyed peas where there was room.

She looked at him before she returned to the stove.

"There's hot coffee on the stove," she pointed.

He smiled and nodded. "Thank you, ma'am."

The men lagging outside began to file in and fill the empty spaces at the table. One, a middle-aged, burly man, ambled over to where Lawrence was seated. He towered above most of the others and spoke to Lawrence condescendingly. "You're in my seat, bud!"

Lawrence's eyes put the clout in his words as he slowly looked up at the big man and spoke. "Maybe you better practice on how to speak to a stranger," he said and slid over.

"Yeah? Well, you best not set in my place again!" the guy demanded.

Mollie looked over her shoulder. "Now, you listen here, Joe! Don't you come in here and start a fight or you can eat outside! And further more, you nor anyone else owns a private place at the table!"

Mollie married Lawrence in the early part of 1911.

Mollie had been blessed with a wonderful personality. She made friends easily and became close friends with a young woman who lived with her husband and little girl four or five miles from the logging camp. One afternoon, Mollie took a little trail that led her to the woman's cabin.

The woman's three-year-old daughter was playing in the timber just outside the cabin when the women heard the child scream. They ran outside and saw a huge cougar walking away with the child locked in his powerful teeth. The fearless women tore after the cougar, screaming in horror. The cougar broke out of his state of leisure, kicking his gait to a lope, and was out of sight before the women had run twenty yards. They didn't give up and followed his tracks. All they ever found of the child was her doll and shreds of her bloody clothing. Unfortunately, in that area the only options of reaching help were limited to walking, riding a horse, or traveling by wagon. There were no telephones. The closest telephone was in town, fifty miles away.

Life was tough for mountain people in those days, and isolation common. When fate struck, it struck wickedly.

Lawrence and Mollie kept working and lived at the logging camp at Florence until that fall, then moved south ten miles to Lake Creek.

On October 15, 1911, Mollie gave birth to their first son, Henry Lawrence (Hank), at Lake Creek.

While Hank was still in diapers, a fire broke out at the head of a canyon above the logging camp at Florence. The fear of forest fires was constant in the timber country. Those who lived there knew it could sweep in and cremate every living thing in its wake.

A savage, west wind had cranked up behind the fire and blasted the roaring flames down the canyon like a runaway freight train. The only escape from the flames was Lake Creek. Terrified and panicked people from every direction were heading straight for the creek. Most were on foot, some on horses. Hundreds of animals—deer, elk, bear, coyotes, wolves, cougars, bobcats, and every small varmint in the vicinity—also fled to the creek and jumped into the slow current with the people, fearing the fire more than the presence of nearby human life.

Mollie had Hank locked in her arms and nearly outran Lawrence to the creek.

The fire burned Mapleton, the town of Lake Creek, Florence, and every cabin in its path to the ground. But the community wasted no time rebuilding. Lawrence and Mollie, their own cabin destroyed, helped the Almasies rebuild, and then they moved to Mapleton.

3

Spencer Butte

Albert Christensen, Mollie and Lawrence's second son, was born in Mapleton in 1913. They named him Albert after an uncle on his father's side.

When the boy was old enough to make his own decisions, he began to think up names that were more compatible with his lifestyle of "huntin', trappin', and ridin'," so he chose Bobby.

In 1921, Lawrence and his family left Mapleton and walked to the old Bailey Hill ranch, twenty or so miles south of Eugene, to live with Grandma Christensen, Lawrence's mother, and his two brothers, Albert, whom Bobby was named after, and George.

While they were living there, Grandad Christensen and his boys were clearing timber one day when a giant tree crushed the old man to death. His end was a case of being in the wrong place at the wrong time. At his age, he was neither alert nor fast enough to outmaneuver his fate.

The streak of having boys ran out for Mollie eight years after Bobby was born. She had her third and final child, a girl they named Martha, at the Bailey Hill place.

Martha also would choose not to go by her given name. She preferred to be called Babe.

Uncle Albert Christensen had no education to speak of but was gifted with a built-in sense of engineering. Albert and George built every structure on the Bailey Hill place. Modern roofed buildings had yet to be used in that part of America at that time. Instead, they were constructed with "A" frame roofs, the purpose being to allow heavy snow to slide off. Some years later, Uncle Albert was killed when he fell off the steep barn roof.

After Lawrence and his brood lived at Bailey Hill for a year, a little place on 125 acres came up for lease, five miles out of Eugene. The acreage was located on part of what had originally been the old George Rinehart homestead ranch. It embraced a parcel of ground on the Jonathan Riggs Donation Land Claim, a lush valley just north of Eugene and at the foot of Spencer Butte, a mountain just to the south. The valley is shown on present-day Oregon maps as "The Christensen Valley."

In the middle 1800s, Rinehart sold out to a man named Brumley. Brumley lost the place to an overdue bank loan. Then Alexander Osburn bought it at a sheriff's sale. Osburn started buying up other homestead claims and ended up with about a 20,000-acre outfit. He put together a dairy and ran over 4,000 head of beef cattle.

The name Spencer Butte, christened so in the early 1800s, resulted from an encounter between two government scouts and a band of renegade Oglalla Sioux. Using flintlock rifles in a running shootout, the scouts outran the Indians and took refuge in a shallow cave in the rocks at the top of a butte on the mountain range. They held the renegades off for two days and finally killed them all. One of the scouts was named Spencer; thus the name Spencer Butte.

Grandma had given Lawrence and Mollie an old wagon, a team of horses, and one cow. Other than their clothes and a few belongings, that was the extent of their holdings when they started their move to the valley.

The 125 acres that had come up for rent included a pretty

good house and barn and a good set of corrals. Frank Chambers owned it then. A big milking barn, creamery, and cheese press and a weathered old dairy barn standing near a rundown set of cattle pens were the remnants of a dairy that had been there early on. Floating legends say it was a cover for a moonshining operation.

They had made the 'shine in the cellar. The stovepipe from the still ran to the fireplace upstairs, and most of the smoke from the chimney resulted from mash cooking. It was a regular moonshine den. Probably no one would have given a second thought to the possibility that the smoke might not be wood burning.

Bullet-riddled doors and birdshot-peppered walls established solid evidence of a long-ago shootout. The story goes that the shootout was with the law—and the law won! One moonshiner was killed, and another's leg was shot off.

The house sat on the side of a gradual little slope below Spencer Butte. A live creek split a big meadow that spread across to a long ridge covered with fir trees, scrub oak, and manzanita.

When the family went to town, Lawrence would load the kids in the back of the wagon. Mollie sat on the high seat with Lawrence. The wagon had no tailgate, making it perfect for the kids to hang their legs off.

Every week or two the wheels would begin wobbling. Lawrence would pull the wheels and throw them into the creek to soak. The water and warmth of the sun would swell the hubs, and they would fit on the axles for another ten trips.

The original Almasie family had scattered. Grandpa Almasie (Michael) and Grandma (Suzy) had built a two-story home in Lake Creek. Mollie often took her children into Lake Creek to be with her mother and sisters. Anna and her only child, a sixteen-year-old girl, were there. Beth was married and raised three children in southern California, and Andrew and Joe had moved to San Francisco and started a contracting business, building fashionable homes. They were both married with grown children.

Grandpa Almasie (Michael) died in 1921. The closest mortuary was in Eugene, some fifty odd miles from Lake Creek. To get Michael's body to Eugene, it would have to be sent by train.

Unfortunately, the train only passed through Lake Creek once a week. Therefore the body was kept in the attic. Mollie had Bobby sit with it for that week, a chilling experience for an eight-year-old.

The economy began to slow down in the winter of '28. Work was getting scarce everywhere, and the depression stormed in like a hurricane in '29. The bottom fell out of the stock market back east, like a swatted fly falling off a windowpane. No one had money, excluding the very wealthy. A common man couldn't buy a job. There were none to be had. City streets were long with bread lines and short on luxuries. Country folks had to rely on their skills to manage, and not all of them had the kind of skills it took. There was plenty of game, but hardly anyone had enough money to buy shells.

Lawrence had managed to get two big workhorses to farm with before the depression, and he sold a little of what he grew. Mollie canned what he didn't sell and raised a few turkeys, and thus the Christensens got along.

Bobby trapped on the way to and from school and in the summer when he wasn't working on the ranch. In those years he couldn't catch much of anything but skunks and a few small creatures that were looking for a handy meal. He was able to get a quarter a piece for the skunk hides. For a kid, that was big money in the depression. Every now and then he'd catch a mink. Mink hides brought big money, $10-12 apiece.

It seemed to the kids like everybody in the country was starving. The Christensens were far from getting fat and sassy, but they were doing pretty good, with the farming, Mollie's turkey money, and whatever Bobby made on his hides.

A neighbor, Mr. Kirkpatrick, farmed pumpkins on a few acres near Creswell, some ten miles south of Eugene. The pulp in the big gourd-like fruit could have been solid gold and he still couldn't have sold it. The pumpkin business had crashed right along with the stock market. Kirkpatrick scavenged the country for work. There was nothing. After the last door slammed in his face, he found himself on the brink of murder. He had to get food to feed nine children, a wife, and a wrinkled grandmother.

One afternoon in his search for work Kirkpatrick met Bobby on the trail. Bobby had just run his traps and was toting two skunk hides. Kirkpatrick asked the boy if he might give him the fat off his skunk hides. He didn't have enough money to buy lard and needed the skunk fat to fry his pumpkins, he said, so Bobby gave him all the skunk hides he could spare. The Kirkpatricks were awfully poor, but so were most other folks.

The little country schools had only one room, and the teachers would have to control and teach grades one through eight. There were no school buses. Even if there had been, the state couldn't have afforded to run them. So the kids walked to school. Some of the little ones would come to school with nothing to eat except maybe a little parched corn in their pockets. The Christensen children, like the majority of other children, had been taught to share, and Mollie sent extra lunch with them.

It was really tough on kids, especially ones like the Kirkpatrick kids.

Bobby quit school, but Hank and Babe were determined to graduate and go to college. There was no sitting around on the Christensen ranch, and Bobby knew when he dropped out of high school he'd have to pour it on from sunup to sundown. Lawrence had a saying: "If you don't work, you'll wear out your pockets diggin' for money that ain't there."

Lawrence had taught Bobby to shoot while his young spirit was still tame. He was an expert marksman and did the hunting for the family. Bullets were too expensive to waste with the depression going on, so when Bobby hunted he'd only take one shell.

After he loaded his .30-30 one morning and whistled up his dog, Rex, they struck out to get a deer. The hike up Spencer Butte was a good vertical climb through pines with arms limb to limb. It wasn't long before Rex caught scent of a big buck, stopped dead still, sniffed in the air, and lit out.

Bobby couldn't see him but could hear him barking like an Arkansas coon dog as he dashed through the brush. Bobby knew he was on a deer and levered the shell in his carbine. It was too thick for Bobby to get a shot, so he got on the tracks in a Tennessee trot.

Rex ran the buck until he winded him, then made a beeline back to Bobby and led him to where he could get his sights on the buck. Bobby downed him with the only bullet he had.

4

Edgar Buchanan and His Traveling Trio

The first time Bobby saw Rex, he knew he was a smart dog. But when he began teaching him, he realized Rex wasn't just smart—he was extremely intelligent.

Bobby taught him to do all kinds of tricks. In no time he could climb a thirty-foot ladder with a flag in his mouth. Bobby built a little platform on the ladder for a place for Rex to stand after he reached the top. When his master signaled his cue, the little dog would jump, and down he'd come with his ears and tail blowing straight up. Bobby, Hank, and Babe had a canvas tarp ready for the landing.

He learned to get wood in for Mollie and did so in the following manner. The firewood was in a small, fenced-in area. Rex would trot to the gate, slide the wooden latch back with his nose, and push the gate open. He would get a stick from the wood pile with his teeth, carry it out the gate, drop it on the ground, push the gate closed, latch it (with his nose, of course), then pick up the stick and take it to the house. If the door was shut, he'd tap it with the stick and Mollie would let him in. Wagging his tail every step, he'd trot to the wood box, drop the stick in it, and hustle right back to get another one. He would keep up the routine until the wood box was full.

Rex was a regular ham and loved learning anything to earn him praise. There was only one trick he dreaded—smoking a cigarette!

Bobby didn't smoke, but Lawrence and Hank did. When Bobby told Rex to smoke a cigarette, he'd look up at Bobby, speaking with his drooping eyes. "Do I have to?" Bobby would point at Lawrence or Hank, and Rex would trot over so that one of them would put a cigarette in his mouth. He didn't take to it, but he'd trot back to Bobby with his head cocked and his nose wrinkled up, trying to keep from smelling the cigarette.

He could ride a horse, too. Bobby taught him to sit up in the saddle and hold the bridle reins in his mouth. When asked if he was sick, Rex would sneeze and paw at his nose.

In 1925, when Bobby was twelve years old, he heard that Rin-Tin-Tin, the famous movie dog, was appearing at the state fair in Salem. He took Rex, along with a little of his skunk money, and headed for Eugene on foot and hitched a ride to Salem. After they reached Salem and found the man in charge of entertainment at the fair, Bobby told him that Rex could outdo ol' Rin-Tin-Tin any day of the week.

"Is that so? He don't look smart enough to do anything but wag his tail," the man said, but agreed to let Rex audition.

The man was smoking a cigar. Bobby had to ask him if he would let Rex show him he could smoke it.

"Well, I'll be darned," the man said when Bobby put the cigar in the dog's mouth and he held it until Bobby took it out.

Back home, Lawrence wouldn't budge at first, but when Bobby told him that he had to take the ladder for Rex to climb, he sort of grumbled and nodded his head, agreeing to take them to the fair the next day.

The grandstand was packed with people when Rex climbed the ladder and jumped in the tarp. The crowd went wild.

Edgar Buchanan, a dentist in Eugene, put on a little free variety show every Sunday afternoon at the feed mill for the kids.

Someone had told him about Rex, after the fair, and he drove out to the ranch one day and found Lawrence plowing.

"Good afternoon, sir," he said when Lawrence stopped the team. Bobby was standing nearby. "They tell me your boy has the smartest dog in the country."

Lawrence pulled his bandanna out of his hip pocket and wiped his forehead. They shook when Buchanan offered his hand.

"The name's Buchanan—Edgar Buchanan."

Lawrence nodded his head. "Lawrence Christensen. Now, what was it you wanted?"

"I got wind that your boy's got a real smart dog," Buchanan answered.

Lawrence shrugged his shoulders.

"They say he's the smartest dog in the country."

"I don't know about that," Lawrence said. "But he can do a few tricks, all right."

Both men were wearing bib overalls. Buchanan took his Days Work out of his pocket and offered a plug to Lawrence.

"If it'd be all right," Buchanan began, "I'd like to have the lad get that dog to show me some tricks."

"I reckon that'll be just fine," Lawrence said and looked at Bobby. Bobby had known right off who Edgar Buchanan was.

"I'd like to see your dog do some tricks, son," Buchanan said, offering his hand to Bobby. After they shook, Bobby just stood there with his eyes glued on Buchanan.

"Well, don't just stand there, son," Lawrence said. "Take Mr. Buchanan up to the house and show 'em what Rex can do!"

Buchanan and Bobby walked to the house. Bobby whistled Rex out from under the porch and had him do some tricks.

"By golly, he's somethin', all right," Buchanan said with a compliment in his tone. "How'd you like to put him in my show? I'm goin' on the road in a few days, and I think you and Rex are just what I need."

Bobby was tickled to death when Lawrence and Mollie told him it would be fine.

The day before the tour started, Bobby managed to get Rex

The Saga of the Legendary Christensen Family 27

in a water trough and bathe him. Rex took to the water like a duck, but he didn't take to the sudsy stuff. It was a rodeo to get him bathed. Bobby was soaked to the skin when Babe yelled from the house, "Your water's hot, Bobby!" Everyone in the family bathed in a number-three washtub in front of the kitchen stove, and that is where Bobby headed to get clean.

He didn't sleep much that night, his mind being on show business.

The next morning he beat daylight up and joined Mollie and Lawrence over coffee in the kitchen. Then Mollie packed some clothes for him. Buchanan arrived at the ranch about ten o'clock, driving a long, black touring car. Buchanan had already employed two young girls who sang and danced, and they were both pretty.

The car was a beautiful piece of machinery, equipped with a radio and heater, luxurious conveniences in the Charleston era. Touring cars such as this one had no top for the chauffeur.

Bobby told Buchanan that he'd gladly do the driving. Buchanan spat tobacco juice and told Bobby that he'd do the driving.

There were no such things as motels in those days. People stayed in places called auto-courts. Motels weren't introduced until a few years later, in the thirties. The first known motel (motor hotel) was built in Santa Barbara, California, after Route 66 was built. People didn't start calling roadside inns "motels" until after the Second World War.

Unfortunately, the shows didn't make enough profit for them to afford hotel rooms, so they would pitch camp wherever they were and sleep in bedrolls. The girls cooked on a campfire and did a good job of it.

They toured throughout southern Oregon and northern California for a few weeks, but the show flopped. Buchanan sold the touring car to catch up on his rent after he took Bobby and the girls back to Eugene.

In the thirties, Edgar Buchanan went to work doing bit parts in the movies and later landed a starring role in the television show, *Petticoat Junction*.

5

The Three Sisters

One Saturday afternoon when Hank and Bobby were in town to go to a movie, they went into Clem's Store to look around. Clem's carried clothing and all kind of tools: hammers, nails, monkey wrenches, posthole diggers, barbed wire, wire-pliers, wire-staples, pocketknives, saddles, bridles, horseshoes, and harness. Everything to do with horses, except wagons. You name it, chances are they had it. They even sold goodies: horehound, jawbreakers, licorice, jellybeans, peanuts, and walnuts. There was always a sale sign in the store window, reading:

Genuine Levi Strauss britches.
Top of the line Acme and Blucher cowboy boots.
Western shirts and Stetson hats. All on sale.

Hank and Bobby were more interested in the saddles than any of the merchandise. Most of the saddles were on the cheap side, but that day there was a good one, a Hamley.

While they were looking it over, they overheard a customer telling someone else that the Forest Service was looking for a man who could handle a string of packhorses and trap. That was right up Bobby's alley, so he strutted up to the two men like he owned the place.

"I can handle a pack string and trap," he stated boldly. "Who do I talk to about getting the job?"

The customer answered, "Elliot Ballard, the head forest ranger. You can see him tomorrow at the Forest Service office. But you better know what you're doin'. He ain't the easiest man in the country to work for!"

Bobby left Hank in town. He was too excited about the job to stick around, and lit out for home in a high lope.

When he reached the ranch, he passed Babe in the yard playing with her doll and took two porch steps at a time, nearly ripping the screen door off the hinges when he burst into the kitchen. Mollie was sweeping the floor.

"My Lord, Bobby, don't tear the house down!" she said.

Bobby was gasping for air.

Mollie stopped sweeping. "What in the world's wrong? Where's Hank?"

"Nothin's wrong, Mom!" Bobby answered. "I'm goin' to work, packin' and trappin' for the Forest Service."

"That's real nice, son. Now where's Hank?" Mollie asked.

"I'll probably start tomorrow!"

Mollie squinted at him. That was a bad sign.

"Okay, Bobby, where's Hank?" she insisted.

Bobby slipped over and kissed her cheek, pulled the broom out of her hand, and started dancing with it.

"Give me that broom!" she ordered.

Lawrence entered the kitchen. "Who's your dancin' partner, son?"

Bobby settled down and told his news in slight exaggeration.

"How much are they gonna pay ya?" Lawrence asked.

"I'll find out tomorrow when I go down and tell Mr. Elliot Ballard I want the job."

"Now, that was good thinkin', son," Lawrence said proudly. "It's usually best to tell a man you'll give it some thought before you make up your mind to take a job and ask what the pay is."

"What time is your appointment?" Mollie asked.

When Bobby said he had only heard about the job, Mollie gave him a good scolding for lying earlier. But Lawrence took his side and said it wasn't exactly a lie. "He was just a little overconfident, Mother."

Mollie bristled and continued sweeping.

When Lawrence and Bobby headed for the door, Mollie once more asked Bobby where Hank was, making certain he heard her. He told her Hank went to the picture show.

Bobby walked to the U.S. Forest Service building in Eugene the next morning. Bobby told the receptionist, a middle-aged woman, that he was there to see Ranger Elliot Ballard about the job.

"Do you have experience?" she asked.

"Yes, ma'am, I sure do. I've been packin' and trappin' since I was a kid."

She looked him over and smiled. "You still look like a kid to me."

About that time, Elliot entered the room from the hall. The receptionist told him that Bobby was there about the job. Elliot led the way to his office. When they were in the room, Elliot began looking over a map on the wall.

Bobby stood there for five minutes before Elliot spoke. "Well, don't just stand there—sit down! Can't you see that chair right in front of you?" Elliot said in a gruff voice. Bobby didn't have time to answer him before he spoke again. "So you think you're a packer, huh? How old are you?"

Bobby told him he was fifteen.

"What's your name?" Elliot asked. After Bobby told him, the ranger looked around and spoke in a pleasant tone. "Are you one of Lawrence and Mollie Christensen's boys?"

As soon as Bobby told him he was, that was the end of the interview.

"You better bring along your traps, if you got any," Elliot said. "And bring a gun and shells, and a dog if you got one."

On the way home, Bobby thought about taking Rex, but he

knew Rex wasn't a coyote and cougar dog. So the next morning, after he loaded his outfit in the family's old car, he whistled and a bloodhound named Crowbar came running up. Crowbar wasn't the best dog Bobby ever owned, but he'd do. Lawrence got Bobby to the ranger office by 8:00 A.M.

While Lawrence and Elliot visited, Bobby took his stuff out of the car and lugged it to a hard-used, green, 1928 flatbed Forest Service truck. A long, topless wooden trailer was hooked to the truck, with six packhorses, a big mule, and two saddle horses in it.

Elliot yelled for Bobby to throw his outfit into the bed of the truck. His outfit consisted of his saddle, his chaps, a cowboy bed, a gunnysack full of clothes, and one full of traps. He tied his bridle and spurs to the saddle.

Crowbar had to ride on the floor in the cab and didn't have enough room to scratch. It was the middle of June, and, needless to say, it was hot.

Elliot had the windshield cranked out, and the windows and wind-wings were wide open. With the wind whipping in all the windows, mixing with the rattling fenders, Bobby couldn't have heard Elliot say a thing if he would have. But he didn't, so it didn't matter.

The firewall was thin, and poor Crowbar was roasting on the floor, slobbering all over Bobby's boots.

They were knocking down about twenty-five miles an hour, headed east on 116, a narrow gravel road. At Walterville they crossed the Mackenzie on a one-lane bridge and stayed along the river, passing through Leaburg, Vida, and Finn Rock, and then crossing the south fork of the Mackenzie again just east of Blue River.

Elliot began to slow down as they neared a turn-off. The little road they took highly resembled a cow trail and was just as rough as it was crooked. Bobby bounced around like he was doing the Saint Vitus dance. Elliot had the steering wheel to hold him down. They were in the Cascade Range. Elliot was quiet, crafting the noisy truck along for a couple of more slow miles. He looked over at Bobby. "She's a little rough, ain't she, son? And she gets worse."

The magnificent Three Sisters watched the truck and trailer rock slowly across the timbered wilderness toward the pack station at Horse Creek. The little station was tucked snug in a quiet meadow, lost among soaring green pine and juniper.

Bobby was dozing when Crowbar suddenly sat up, howling. Bobby nearly jumped out of his hide. This made Elliot laugh so hard he could hardly keep the truck on the road.

It became a three-ring circus: Elliot and Bobby in stitches, with Crowbar howling like he had a wounded bear treed. Elliot had to stop the truck so Bobby could shut Crowbar up.

In a short time the road dead-ended at the pack station (base camp). It was long after the sun had fallen asleep, and the night air was chilly enough for them to put on their Levi jackets.

The pack station consisted of a one-room cabin, a shed, and a pole corral with an unloading chute. The outside toilet had the letters USFS stenciled on the door.

It was too late for Elliot to head back after they unloaded the horses, so he would stay the night.

There was a cot in the cabin, all made up, that Elliot slept on. Bobby rolled his bed out on the floor. He was so tired he could hardly undress. By the time he was in bed, Elliot was snoring so loudly he couldn't go to sleep. Bobby tossed and turned until he could take no more and packed his bed outside. He moved far enough away from the cabin so he couldn't hear Elliot snore through the walls and was asleep by the time he was under his quilts.

The next morning Elliot cooked up a little breakfast. After they ate, he showed Bobby a stack of eight-foot 2x4s and a stack of ready-made twelve-foot-long rafters.

"The rafters are too heavy for the horses, so you'll have to pack them on the mule," Elliot said. "We're building a cabin at the Lookout on the Sisters." He pointed at the Middle Mountain of the Three Sisters.

The sawbucks were in the little shed with the grain. Elliot watched how Bobby put them on the string of horses and was apparently satisfied; he didn't say anything one way or the other.

"I'll help you get loaded for this trip," Elliot said. "It takes two men to sling the rafters. I'll have a man here to help you tomorrow." He told Bobby he needn't tie the mule in the string of horses; the mule would follow along and keep up.

The first thing Bobby did before they started to load the lumber was to pull off his jacket. It took a good hour before they had the pack string ready. Bobby got on his horse.

"When you reach the Middle Sister, the trail's narrow and steep," Elliot said, pointing out the trail. "Be damned careful and take your time," he continued. "It's twenty-six miles to the Lookout. It'll be dark when you get there, but there's a crew there so you'll have plenty of help to unload. You can head back here in the morning."

Bobby nodded so long to Elliot, whistled at Crowbar, and started up the trail.

Before long the camp was out of sight. The timber was so tall it looked as though it could poke a hole through the clouds. The grass was belly deep to the horses. Indian paintbrushes blended with a rainbow of wildflowers growing everywhere.

The pack string was stretched out behind Bobby's saddle horse. The big mule stole bites of grass as he moved along. The trail snaked along for ten or so miles before it reached the hem of the Middle Sister's skirt.

The switchbacks were rocky and steep. The horses had no trouble making the turns, but the cumbersome rafters on the mule stuck out two feet on both ends and he had to creep around the switchbacks with extreme caution. Every now and then, Bobby would hear the rafters scrape. He'd look back to see if things were all right.

Every once in a while Crowbar would reveal himself trotting through the timber or stopped with a back leg hiked up a tree.

It was dark when Bobby finally spotted a lamp flickering through the trees and knew there was someone awake at the Lookout to help him unload the lumber. When the chore was over, the cook rustled him up some hot grub. After a good night's sleep he was back on the trail to base camp before daylight. The trip back was much faster.

When he reached base camp that afternoon, he unsaddled and grained the horses before going into the cabin.

Pete's bare feet were hanging off the end of the cot. It was the first Bobby ever saw him. He was out like a light. Elliot had brought him that morning to help Bobby. Crowbar snuck in before Bobby got the door shut behind him and began to bark. Pete shot straight up and leaped to the floor, wide-eyed and bushy-tailed.

Bobby quieted Crowbar and shook hands with Pete.

The long-legged, middle-aged German had brought his accent along from the old country. It was difficult for Bobby to understand him, but they got acquainted.

Pete was an excellent horse-shoer, a top-notch packer, and was light on a horse's mouth. And besides being a top hand, he had a broad smile and a sense of humor. He was constantly tamping Bobby full of funny stories and good jokes. They took turns packing the lumber.

On the days Bobby stayed at base camp, he ran his traps along the Mackenzie. The country was bursting wide open with game. Within two weeks he caught three wolverines, one lynx, a badger, a red fox, and seven coyotes.

Pete had just finished shoeing the last foot on a packhorse one morning when a kid just older than Bobby drove up in the flatbed truck with the same trailer in tow. He was there to take Bobby and Pete to a hot spot blazing along the Rouge River in the wilderness, three or four miles east of Bald Knob.

Elliot had just hired the boy. The Forest Service was hiring anyone they could find.

When the fire season started, burns began to break out everywhere in the Coast Mountain Range. A catastrophic wind out of Canada was driving the flames. The Rouge River was nearly 200 miles southwest of Horse Creek the way the crow flies.

They had to backtrack and cross the Mackenzie at Blue River, then head south on a Forest Service road that ran along the south fork. Within fifteen miles they crossed over to the east side again and crossed back to the west side in about four more miles. They turned due west to Wester, crossed the north fork of the Willamette at Oakridge, traveled south thirty miles and crossed the middle fork of the Willamette, then bumped along for another thirty-five miles to Toketee Falls. There they crossed the Umpqua. Tiller was around eighty miles on southwest, and they hit a dead end there at a county road that took them northwest, passing Milo and on to Day's Creek, where they crossed the south fork of the Umpqua.

They continued on and soon rolled through Canyonville, turned northwest to Riddle, crossed the Crow Creek, followed it to a plateau spread from the foot of Dutchman Butte, and hit another forest road that ended at a temporary camp Elliot had set up. There were eight extra horses in the corral.

When they had the horses unloaded, the kid left. It was too close to dark and too late to pack supplies to the firefighter, so they tacked shoes on two horses. After finishing that chore, Pete brewed a pot of coffee and cooked up some steak and frijoles. Bobby handled the potato-peeling chore and washed the dishes.

It was dark when they fed the horses. Being short two feedbags, Pete made two *morrales* out of gunnysacks, filled them with grain, and hung them on the two horses. Bobby had never seen a *morrale* and told Pete that it was a clever idea. Pete told Bobby that he had once seen a Mexican man make one, and the homemade feedbags were all the vaqueros used to grain their ponies in Mexico.

At first light the next morning they were up, dressed, and full of bacon, eggs, biscuits and gravy, and coffee. The forest fire was burning deep in the mountains to the west, hiding Bald Knob with smoke.

Pete packed his string with fire-fighting tools and two boxes of dynamite and headed out. Bobby had his string loaded with grub, threw a diamond hitch on the mule, whistled at Crowbar, and was ready to battle the mountains and canyons.

Pete's tracks were following a little game trail chiseled out on the steep slope of a timber-covered mountain and crawled along the rim of the Rouge River Canyon. It was at least a 300-foot drop to the river—a breathtaking sight.

All of a sudden Bobby heard the mule braying for all he was worth. Bobby stopped the horses and looked back. A swarm of hornets were all over the mule. He was running and bucking straight for the horses, his pack dragging and scattering groceries everywhere. Before Bobby could untrack the horses, the mule dove under the last horse in the string and drove him straight off the edge. He took four horses with him. If the rope hadn't snapped on Bobby's lead horse, the whole bunch would have gone, including Bobby. He could hear the horses crashing down the canyon wall as he held a death grip on the saddlehorn. Butterflies were playing tag in his stomach when he eased off his horse and looked in the canyon.

The mule was shutdown right on the edge. The hornets had scattered in the wreck. Two horses landed in the river and were dead. The other three landed on a wide ledge, kind of a little plateau that stuck out about forty feet down. They were skinned up but alive. All the grub Bobby had now was on the only packhorse he had left.

Bobby's heart never stopped pounding until he topped out in a big open meadow. He pulled up to let the horses and the mule blow.

With all the fires going it would take at least a month before they could get a trail built for the stranded horses, but it was critical for Bobby and Pete to keep supplies moving. Elliot hired a temporary man to get hay and water to the marooned horses. The extra man packed a bale of hay a day. When he reached the rim of the canyon he pushed the hay over the edge to the stranded horses. He packed five ten-gallon cans of water a week, poured them into a barrel, and lowered it down on a rope. Eventually they would build the trail for the horses and get them off the mountain.

The fire season was over in the fall. Elliot laid off Pete and put Bobby at the Lookout on Middle Sister. Bobby was thrilled with that arrangement. The new cabin was well insulated and couldn't have been cozier for the winter. He had three fat saddle horses and plenty of grain to keep them that way through the winter. There was a shed full of firewood for the potbelly in the cabin, and an abundance of game to hunt as well as plenty of .30-30 shells. Crowbar would be fine company.

One afternoon it began snowing. By night a good two inches had fallen. Bobby was in no hurry to go to the outhouse when he woke up at 2:00 in the morning. He waited until he could hold it no longer. Being in no mood to put on his Levis and boots, he settled for his jacket and slippers instead and ventured outside in his longhandles.

Crowbar always trotted up when Bobby came out of the cabin, but he didn't show that time. Bobby figured he was hid out someplace to get out of the weather.

When he got the snow kicked away from the outhouse door to open it, Bobby heard something bawling like a cow and caught site of Crowbar bouncing across an open, snow-covered meadow, barking with all he had. He assured himself the dog was probably after a rabbit, so he went back to bed.

There was no reason for him to get up before daylight the next morning. The sun was up when he started a pot of coffee, put a couple of sticks of wood in the potbelly, and let the revived fire heat his backside while he waited for the coffee to boil.

The only bad thing about being alone was that he missed his mother and Pete's cooking. He could get by on his own, though. While he was eating bacon and eggs, he began to wonder why Crowbar hadn't scratched on the door. He knew there had to be something wrong. After he cleaned up his mess he bundled up, saddled a horse, and struck out to find him. He had no trouble tracking him through the snow.

Steam was fogging from the horse's nostrils. Bobby stopped at intervals so he could blow. The closer they got to North Sister, where the snow was growing deeper, the harder the horse had to work. Bobby rode until he hit two sets of paw tracks. He stayed on the sign until he found a spot where the snow was blood red and torn up. There had been a scrap. Tracks and blood drops were leading on. Bobby picked up his horse's head to follow the tracks and noticed a portion of Crowbar's collar sticking out of the snow. He dismounted and kicked around in the snow, but didn't uncover so much as one dog hair. Either a cougar or a wolf had killed him and carried him off for the feast.

Elliot rode to the Lookout in late October to check on Bobby and to let him know he had Christmas off. He said there would be someone at Horse Creek to pick him up Christmas Eve morning. Bobby told him about Crowbar and said he guessed he would quit at Christmas, but he would help through the fire season again if he could get away from the ranch.

6

The Origin of the Christensen Brothers Rodeo

Bobby got home on Christmas Eve of 1929, and with the depression on, the holidays were pretty lean. Mollie made a couple of shirts for Lawrence and the boys and three dresses for Babe. Because Babe was only eight, she also got a dollhouse. Hank brought a set of jacks home for her and Bobby had whittled her a little wooden horse. Those things made it a special Christmas.

The following spring was extra wet. Between what the ranch made and what Mollie made with her turkeys, Lawrence had been able buy a steer or horse now and then, and by summer the ranch had a few mama cows with sucking calves, ten or twelve steers, and five workhorses.

Mollie orchestrated the whole outfit and made sure every visitor who came by had a place to sleep and three meals a day. And she worked like a man when it came up.

There was one time when the tractor broke down and no men were around, so she figured out a way to hook the plows to the car and plowed the field. She was a strong-willed, godly woman, and the backbone of the Christensen family.

Every chance they got, Hank and Bobby would ride the steers. The horses were all broke to harness but not to ride. All of them big and stout, they probably would have been rank under a saddle!

When they branded, Bobby got to do most of the roping. He was deadly with a rope; no one ever had to wait for him to drag a calf to the fire. Lawrence and Hank stayed busy on the ground. Babe tended the irons and Mollie often helped. Hank was as stout as a mule and could flank calves with anybody. They branded the C backward B on the left hip of the cattle and earmarked with a swallow fork in the left and the seven under bit in the right. They also branded their horses with a little C backward B on the left shoulder.

One day as they were branding, a man by the name of Hutchinson, who owned a bicycle shop in town, rode up with a young man named Sailor Watkins and ten or twelve kids, all on bicycles. When they reached the corral they climbed off their bicycles and perched on the fence to watch.

When the branding was over, Mr. Hutchinson told Lawrence some of the kids wanted to try their hand at riding the steers. Lawrence didn't mind, and told Hank and Bobby to give them a hand. Bobby loped down to the pasture and brought the steers up.

Sailor Watkins was a wrestler and was teaching a few kids to wrestle. One of them boasted that he could ride any steer. He was a big, rosy-cheeked kid who bullied his way around town. Hank and Bobby were anxious to see him get popped off.

Most of the steers weren't hard to ride. Bobby roped a big one and dragged him to the middle of the pasture. Hank tied a hondo in the end of a cotton rope so they could put it on him.

When the town bully was on the steer, he put both hands under the rope. Babe was there and called out to the kid: "I thought you said you could ride! My brothers ride with one hand! Are you chicken to ride with one hand?"

The lad wasn't ashamed to use both hands and squeezed the rope until his knuckles were white. There was no doubt he was scared out of his wits. He looked like he was about to pee in his britches.

On the first jump the boy's hands came out from under the rope. He bounced up on the steer's neck and hung on like a leech. The poor old steer couldn't buck much with all that weight hanging on his neck. About all he could do was kick at his belly and flounder across the pasture. He drove his front feet in the ground when he stopped at the fence, and the boy sailed off, landing on the top wire of the fence.

None of the kids felt bad about laughing. The boy only had a shallow cut or two on his belly, and his shirt was ripped half off. But he was much more scared than he was hurt.

That day was the start of the Christensen Brothers rodeo business. Mr. Hutchinson and Sailor Watkins would bring kids out a couple more times, and then the kids started coming by themselves. They would come every Sunday and bring more with them. Before long, all kind of folks were showing up.

Mollie told her sons they should start charging a dime admission. So they did.

One of the horses was a big work mare that was double rank. One afternoon Hank and Bobby tried her out, and she almost sent them both to the moon. Lawrence was there. Hank tried her first, and Lawrence bent over laughing and slapping his leg when she threw Hank.

"By damn, that hag can pitch!" Lawrence said. "If I was you boys I'd take 'er to the rodeo in Salem next week and see if I could sell 'er to that Callahan outfit. I'll bet Callahan would give you fifty for 'er without battin' an eye."

"We're gonna keep her to practice on, Pop," Hank said.

Twenty dollars would buy a decent bucking horse in those days, and twenty-five would buy a damn good one. When one came along that could throw off the champions, it would bring up to fifty dollars.

"You'd be smart to sell 'er," Lawrence continued. "If she brings fifty you can buy two good cheap ones to practice on. You can't neither one ride her nohow."

"I'll bet I can, by darn!" Bobby boasted.

"You couldn't ride her strapped in a washtub!" Hank laughed.

"Yeah? We'll just see about that!" Bobby shot back.

Bobby was sixteen now and thought he could ride anything with hair on it.

"All right, Hot Shot!" Hank said. "Get your saddle and lace it on her."

Bobby didn't have any trouble catching the mare, as she was halter broke and gentle, but he had to be easy with her when he buckled on the flank. As he pulled his hat down and started to climb on her, he realized she was much taller than he had thought. Hank had had no trouble getting on her, but Bobby was a bench-legged kid. Hank had to leg him up. The mare stood quietly while Bobby planted his feet in the stirrups.

"You better screw down real tight and scoot under the swells, Hot Shot," Hank said, "or you won't get past the first jump when she kicks off the lid. You probably won't ride her three jumps anyway!"

Bobby was going to show Hank what a real bronc ride looked like, but to his great surprise he only lasted four jumps. At least that was a jump more than Hank had said he would. Bobby had been bucked off plenty of times, but never as hard nor as easily as when that big mare did it.

Lawrence and Hank were both bent over laughing when Bobby got up and knocked the dust off. That did it! Bobby wasn't about to let them get the last laugh. He told them that if they wanted to see him try her again, they'd get the chance in about twenty minutes. He stomped out the gate to work on a plan.

Rex met him and they headed to the timber in a trot. There was plenty of sap in the first big fir tree they came to, and Bobby dug out his pocketknife to pry out enough to rosin his chaps up good.

Despite his efforts, Lawrence and Hank got the last laugh anyway. The mare didn't dampen Bobby's salt, but she drove his head into the dirt again.

"You'd better practice on a milk cow before you pop off again," Hank said.

"Both of you better practice on somethin' you can ride," Lawrence advised. "This mare's way too tough for ya. The best place for her is with a big rodeo outfit, so you'd better saddle up and take 'er to Salem in the mornin'."

Lawrence had a point. The boys decided they'd take the mare to Salem.

The next morning, after they caught her and were saddling their saddle horses, Lawrence walked into the corral.

"Now, don't let 'er jerk aloose from ya and run off, boys," Lawrence said. "There's a lotta country between here and Salem. And by gosh, don't take less than fifty for 'er, neither!"

"Are you sure we should ask that much for her, Pop?" Hank asked. "I've never heard of a workhorse costing that much."

"Well, she ain't no ordinary workhorse, son," Lawrence said. "She's a buckin' fool!"

It was sixty-five or seventy miles from the ranch to Salem. Hank led the mare partway; Bobby led her the rest.

Salem was one of the bigger rodeos in Oregon, and there would be lots of tough bronc riders there. Hank and Bobby were there a week early, so the mare would have a good rest when Callahan bucked her. They were low on money and had to camp out and get by on one meal a day, bread and red without the trimmings.

"How much you boys think she's worth?" Callahan asked when they discussed selling her to him.

"We figure she's worth top dollar," Hank answered.

"She'd need to be *damn good* before I'd pay top dollar for 'er!" Callahan said.

Jessie Stahl, one of the best black cowboys ever known and by far the best black saddle bronc rider, was working the bronc and bull riding. Bobby had never seen a black cowboy and didn't quite know how to take him at first. He was friendly and offered to share his teepee tent with them to get out of the rain if they didn't mind his color.

"The color of a man's skin don't make him any different than any other man," Bobby said.

"That's right," Hank offered. "A black horse is every bit as good as a white one, ain't he?"

Jessie became one of Hank and Bobby's best friends. They soon found out he wasn't only a good guy, he rode as good as most anybody they'd ever seen.

Jessie was in the same class as today's black calf-roping sensation, Fred Whitfield, as agile as a cat, and just as quick. He stood over six feet and rocked the scales at over 200.

Most everyone in that area had heard about the rodeo at John Day, Oregon, in the twenties, where Jessie took second in the bronc riding when every cowboy there knew he should have won it. He got on an exhibition big rank horse the next day and rode him to a standstill.

There were a lot of world champions at Salem, Paddy Ryan among them. He would try the Christensen mare. After he screwed down, the man snubbing pitched her head to Ryan. She jumped high enough to build a barn under her belly, and Paddy roweled her from the mane line to the cantle. Mud spattered ten feet in the air. When she landed, she tried to kick the crows out of the sky. Ryan finally lost his swells and hit the end of his stirrups. While he pulled himself out of the bog hole, the big mare wiped up the arena.

Hank and Bobby were already counting their money when they found Callahan.

"Your old mare bucks pretty good," he said, puffing his cigar.

"*Pretty good?* You haven't got a horse in your herd that can warm her up!" Hank sparked.

Callahan dug up twenty-five dollars and stuck it out to Hank. "That's all she's worth to me."

"Put another twenty-five with that," Hank said, "and you got yourself the best bronc in the country."

"You're forgettin' somethin', ain't ya, son?" Callahan asked. "The feed bill accounts for the other twenty-five."

"Feed bill?" Hank asked. "We might be young, but we didn't

ride in here on a turnip wagon. The mare was on grass, and even if you would've had her on hay she couldn't have eaten over three bales in a week. A big bale of alfalfa only costs two bits. So you still owe us twenty-four dollars."

Callahan puffed up like a peacock and walked away without another word.

The rain never stopped that day. Bobby and Hank spent the night in Jessie's tent, wanting to stay over and watch him ride the next day. He won part of it on a big fleshy roan.

On the way back to the ranch they named their big mare Whirlwind. She didn't spin when she bucked, but the name sounded pretty tough to two kids.

7

Romance on the Camas Swale

Sonny Tureman kicked in a pretty bad little buckskin bareback horse at Salem that year and won part of the bareback riding.

Sonny Tureman's name would be written into the history of rodeo in the late forties as the 1948 World Champion Bareback Rider. After Hank and Bobby became acquainted with him, he would show up at the ranch every now and then. He had a good sense of humor, loved to play practical jokes, and kept everyone around him laughing. Sonny was honest and generally stayed clean with the law, except he liked to fight a little—and was a buzzsaw when it came to that.

After they had stacked hay all day at the ranch that summer, Sonny told Hank he knew a real pretty girl who lived on a farm over by Creswell. Sonny asked him if he wanted to meet her. Hank was sort of bashful about it, but he was no different from any red-blooded American teenage boy and nodded his head. Sonny winked an eye and said they'd go after supper. He mentioned that the girl preferred guys who dressed in suits. Hank just happened to have one that Mollie had made for him to graduate in. They drove to Creswell in Sonny's car.

Hank was surprised at how pretty the girl was, but was *much* more surprised that she was pregnant. When a burly man pushed past her and stuck a double-barreled shotgun in Hank's face, he froze.

"So you're the jasper that knocked Sally up, huh?"

Sonny jerked Hank around and they scattered. Hank was so spooked that when a blast went off he forgot about the car and smoked out across a field. Shotgun blasts roaring over his trail invaded his eardrums. He raced frantically until he reached Creswell. Sonny was sitting in his car with two other guys and the girl when he got there. They were all in hysterics. The one who had appeared in the doorway with the shotgun was the girl's husband.

What else could Hank do but laugh, too?

A middle-aged couple bought twenty or so acres on Camas Swale, just southwest of the ranch. One morning when Hank and Bobby were making a little circle checking the steers, they discovered there were five head of yearlings missing. They found the place where they had left the pasture and drifted up on Camas Swale.

Hank stepped off his horse and handed the reins to Bobby to hold his horse while he knocked on the newcomers' door to inquire about the yearlings.

"Good morning, ma'am," Hank said, lifting off his hat when a pretty girl about his age answered the door.

"Good morning. Would you like to come in?" Her tone was soft.

Hank forgot all about Bobby and followed the girl in the house. Fifteen minutes passed, then a half-hour. Bobby threw a leg over his horse's neck, pushed his hat back, and waited another twenty minutes.

Hank held the door open for the girl when he finally came out of the house. She had on jeans and boots.

"This is my brother Bobby," Hank said to her when they stepped off the porch. "We'll be right back," he said to Bobby. He and the girl walked away and disappeared behind the house. When they reappeared, the girl was leading a little bay horse.

Bobby was tired of holding Hank's pony and gladly handed him the reins.

When the trio reached the west fork of Live Creek, Bobby and Hank's horses stopped and pulled slack in their reins so they could stretch down to drink.

Bobby watched his horse's ears twitch back and forth as he sucked the slow, drifting creek water. He listened as Hank and the girl visited.

The ride was short and the yearlings were easy to find. Hank and the girl left Bobby to mosey along behind the steers when they stopped near her house and said their goodbyes.

"She's a pretty thing, isn't she?" Hank asked when he caught up with Bobby.

"She ain't too bad. Does she have a name?"

"I introduced her to you," Hank said.

"In a manner of speaking, but you didn't tell me her name," Bobby said.

"It's Helen," Hank said bluntly.

Hank began courting Helen and eventually would marry her. They had one child, Peggy, but the marriage only lasted a couple of years.

Hank didn't have the slightest inclination that he would soon meet his second wife, Patricia Canary, at the Crawfordsville rodeo. Pat was a waitress in her mother's little café in Junction City, where all the cowboys going through would stop to eat. Hank had seen Pat at the café but didn't really meet her until the rodeo.

8

The Fourth of July 1929

With the depression still raging, God only knows how a little whistlestop, no bigger than Crawfordsville, Oregon, could afford to put on a rodeo, but the town fathers approved one.

One evening a car pulled up in front of the ranch house, just as Mollie was serving supper. She sat a bowl of potatoes on the table and walked to the window to look out.

Babe jumped up and ran up next to Mollie, airing her lungs. "It's two men in an old car!"

"Hush up, Babe!" Mollie said and waited for the men to reach the porch. When she opened the door and stepped out on the porch, Babe was trailing close behind.

"Good evening. Won't you come in?" Mollie said hospitably and led the men into the kitchen with Babe on their heels. The two men were dressed up in suits, neckties, shined shoes, and snap-brimmed hats in their hands.

Lawrence stood when Babe closed the door behind her.

"How do you do, Mr. Christensen?" the tallest one said, presenting a hand to Lawrence. "I'm Gibb Beach from over at Crawfordsville."

Lawrence shook his hand.

The other man offered his hand. "Lester Porter, sir."

Lawrence nodded and shook hands with him.

Mollie spoke as she sat a roast on the table. "We have plenty if you gentlemen are hungry."

"No thank you, ma'am." Beach smiled. "We had supper just before we came out. You folks go ahead and eat. We'll wait outside."

"You'll do no such thing!" Her words were superior. "Get two chairs out of the front room, Bobby." Mollie continued. Bobby hustled to the front room and grabbed a couple of ladder-backed chairs and carried them into the kitchen.

As the family ate, Lawrence or Mollie would occasionally say something to the men about the weather or the depression, things unimportant to Bobby and Babe. When they had finished eating they excused themselves from the table, carried their plates to the sink, and went to the front room to listen to the radio. Bobby turned it down so he could hear the conversation in the kitchen in case something important was said.

A few minutes passed before Mollie summoned Bobby back into the kitchen.

"These men want to know if we can furnish them with some bucking horses for the Calipooya Roundup in Crawfordsville the Fourth of July, Bobby," Mollie said. "Your dad said it was up to you and Hank."

"You bet we'll furnish the horses!" Bobby said and looked at Hank. He nodded his head.

The men offered to pay $75 for two days. No one objected.

Mollie had breakfast on the table at 4:30 the following morning. Lawrence was at the table with a cup of coffee in front of him when Hank and Bobby entered the kitchen. Getting up that early was nothing new to them. Now that Babe was in school she had to get up with them, but in the summer Mollie let her sleep until 6:00.

The two coal-oil lamps lit the room. One was sitting on the top of the cookstove for Mollie, the other on the table for Lawrence to read by.

After Hank and Bobby poured themselves a cup of coffee and

sat down, Lawrence looked up from his almanac. "You boys sure enough think them workhorses'll buck?" No man had ever been on the horses, but the brothers said it was worth a try to take them to Crawfordsville.

They were big horses, Belgians and Clydesdales. It was doubtful any of them had ever had a shoe on, and they would snort in your hip pocket if you weren't gentle with them. Their fetlocks and manes were as long as a thief's arm, and their tails were long enough to sweep the dust off a lizard's back.

Hank and Bobby would need more horses to put on the rodeo and set their minds to thought. Lawrence knew a guy who had a slaughterhouse in Redmond, with their same name but spelled Christenson. Lawrence had brought him to the ranch to hunt a couple of times, and he always commented on how much he liked Rex and Crowbar, Bobby's dogs. Both were gone now, but Bobby had replaced Crowbar with a blue tick and Rex with a registered English hunter. Although neither could have ever replaced the sentimental worth of old Rex and Crowbar, they turned out to be two of the best hunting dogs in that part of the country.

Old man Christenson told Bobby if he would give him the dogs he would supply them with all the bucking horses they wanted for two cents a pound. He was paying four cents. He promised to save all the spoiled saddle horses he got in and anything else that was snorty. He said they could try them before they bought them.

It was a good deal, but Bobby hated to give up the dogs. If they were going into the rodeo business, though, they would have to have a lot of bucking horses, and good horses were hard to find. Bobby let him have the dogs, and they made the deal on the horses.

Hank borrowed an old Dodge bobtail with sideboards and they left for Redmond the following week to buy twenty head of the horses. It would take more than two men on horseback to drive the broncs to Crawfordsville, so they chose to take Slim Thomson, a middle-aged hired hand and a good hand with horses. He would be plenty of help.

The following Wednesday they had sawbucks laced on three

packhorses. Bobby filled two panniers with grub and cooking utensils, then hung them on his sawbucks. Hank hoisted two soogans on his packhorse and tied them down with a diamond hitch. Slim packed the other bed and a sleeping tent.

Bobby led off, and the Christensen Brothers were heading for the first rodeo of their sixty years in the rodeo business.

It was just breaking light and the remuda followed his horse. The broncs felt good. They bucked and played before they lined out in a lope.

The men had never been to Crawfordsville on horseback and figured to take a little wagon road that ran along the highway. Hank nearly went for an unexpected ride when his horse bogged his head and made a couple of jumps. But before a wreck scattered the herd, Hank picked the horse's head up and laid the bridle reins across his rump—and that was that. The horse settled down and paid attention from then on.

They stayed on the wagon road until they reached Springfield, crossed the highway on the Willamette River bridge, and came to an old logging road. They stayed on the logging road until they got to Marcola, a little logging town nestled in the mountains. Deep in the mountains they hit an old stage road and followed it until they were over the top.

Crawfordsville sat in a little valley below. It had been a hard ride, but they did it in one day.

The sun was fading to bloody orange when they reached the outskirts of town. They turned the remuda out in a little pasture near the arena and scattered twenty-five bales of hay; the committeemen had left plenty for the horses. The Calipooya River ran through the pasture. They found a place to pitch camp on the riverbank, unsaddled and unpacked the horses, staked them out, and broke three bales of hay for them. It would be dark shortly. Bobby and Slim hustled firewood while Hank unpacked the food and cooking utensils. Following a meal, they hit the sack.

Hank and Bobby were both pretty excited about getting the contract, and they lay awake shooting the breeze about things until Slim told them to quiet down and go to sleep.

It was tough crawling out of the sack early the next morning. Hank was pulling on his boots and Slim had coffee boiled when Bobby staggered out of the tent poking in his shirttail. He filled his lungs with cool mountain air, splashed cold water in his face, and poured a cup of coffee.

They ate breakfast then fed the horses. Lester Porter showed up in fifteen or twenty minutes to help them drive the horses from the pasture and put them in the arena to look it over. The arena had been built with new cut posts and 2x6 boards.

The grand entry started at 2:00. There were all kinds of horse races before they were ready to ride broncs: matched saddle horse races, cowhide races, soda pop races, relay races, boot races, and foot races. Some boys even pulled off their boots and ran like Olympic sprinters.

Since there weren't any chutes, Bobby snubbed the broncs to his saddle horse. The big workhorses were a handful to hold with his little 1,100-pound horse. They all had good stout halters on. Bobby had a short rope tied to his saddlehorn that would slip through the halters to snub the broncs close. The riders climbed on his horse behind him and crawled across to get in the bronc saddle.

It was unreal how the big horses bucked. There were good riders there, but only a few made the whistle.

Bobby was the pickupman and Hank was the arena director. The rodeo was slow, but the committeemen were pleased and told Hank and Bobby they could have the contract every year.

Roy Craft, a reporter for the Eugene paper, wanted to help on the drive back to the ranch. He had a horse that he rode in parades and such, but he was a far cry from a cowboy. He wanted to be one in the worst way. He was like most city guys who think it's all just fun and romantic, but he was a nice guy so they let him help.

Instead of driving the horses back over the mountains, they took them across the Willamette valley. The route was just as far that way but not as tough on the horses.

Craft was from that country and knew how far it was from

Crawfordsville back to Eugene. He said he would be just fine when Hank told him it would be a long, tough ride.

"That's fine," Craft said. "I've ridden a lot."

"Okay," Hank said, "but don't expect to stop and rest or eat. We're not stopping once we get them started."

"You don't have to worry about me, Henry," Craft assured.

Hank had him position his horse near the gate to turn the horses when he and Slim pushed them out of the pasture. Craft was to stay in the drag. Bobby loped around and got in front again.

Craft was all hyped up, whoopin' and yellin' and wavin' his hat in the air. Hank told him to pipe down, that he wasn't driving a herd of cattle.

The horses weren't as high as they were when the brothers brought them, and they left in a good trot, staying in it for three or four miles before slowing to a walk. Craft stayed busy keeping them from stopping to graze every few steps.

Craft made a pretty good hand before he started asking if they could stop and rest.

"Now, I told you we weren't stopping," Hank said. "If you can't take it, we can get along without you."

Craft wasn't too pleased with that and didn't mention it again.

By the time they were halfway to the ranch, Craft could hardly stay awake. He was nodding and weaving in the saddle. Before long, he was leaning way out—about to fall.

When he woke up he stopped his horse and borrowed Hank's lariat rope, tied himself in his saddle, and slept for a few miles.

He might have written an article about it for the paper if Hank or Bobby had done the same in order to get a little sleep. But being as it was him, he let it slide.

Part Two
The CB Cowboys

9

Lost at Sea

At the rodeo in Crawfordsville, there happened to be a couple of men from Reedsport who had come to see what appeal the celebration would have for the public. If it went over, they wanted to have a rodeo in Reedsport.

The rodeo had been a success, and the two men were satisfied one could work in their town. They asked Hank and Bobby if they could furnish the stock.

The two young cowboys told the men to give them a few minutes alone to talk it over.

"We can't drive the horses all the way to Reedsport," Hank said to Bobby when they were a few steps away from the men.

"I'm not sure where Reedsport is. How far is it?" Bobby asked.

"It's over a hundred miles," Hank answered. "Way down on the coast toward Coos Bay."

"We can haul them in the wood truck, can't we?" Bobby asked.

"About all the horses we could get on it would be four head," Hank stated. "We'd need at least fourteen or fifteen head."

Bobby slid his hat off his forehead and scratched. "We could make four trips."

"Hell, we couldn't buy that much gas. That old truck guzzles it down like a thirsty horse sucking water," Hank said. "But maybe we can borrow another truck from somebody."

Bobby agreed, and they told the men they would have at least fourteen head there. The men were satisfied with that, and the Christensen Brothers got their second rodeo contract.

It took Hank about two weeks to locate a truck. It was an old flatbed farm truck with homemade sideboards that stopped two feet short of the cab. The old faded truck wasn't much to look at, but it had a good engine and fair tires, and the twenty-eight-foot bed was oak and plenty solid.

The farmer told Hank he could borrow it if he could get it started. There was no telling how long the truck had sat there. Both windows were down, and the dust was thick on the seat. The knob was gone off the shifting lever, and the driver's side of the seat was ripped to the springs. But Hank got it started and drove it home.

When Hank drove in, Bobby came out of the corral with Ed Lewen, a guy in his twenties from eastern Oregon who was working on the ranch that summer.

"Where'd you find this junker?" Bobby asked as Hank got out of the truck.

"Marcola," Hank answered. "A farmer had it parked out by his barn and told me I could borrow it if I could start it."

Bobby opened the hood to look at the motor and spoke. "Does she run pretty good?"

"Yep," Hank said and continued. "Come and look at the bed. It's solid oak. The racks are, too, and they're good and stout." He led the way to the back of the truck.

Bobby looked up to the top of the racks. "How high you think these are?"

"Eight foot," Hank answered.

"I wonder why they don't come all the way to the cab?" Ed wondered.

"I'll bet they left that space for storage," Bobby said and looked at Hank. "How many do you think it'll haul?"

Hank sized the bed up in his head. "Probably ten, maybe twelve head, don't you think?"

"That sounds about right," Bobby answered. "Ed and me can make it in two trips easy."

Hank left for Reedsport in the car around 3:00 the next morning. Bobby and Ed pulled out right behind him loaded with eleven broncs; Whirlwind was in the bunch. Hank was out of sight before Bobby and Ed left the ranch property. Ed was driving. They took state highway 99 to coastal highway 126 and went south. Highway 101 ran right along the shoreline of the Pacific Ocean. It was barely daylight when they hit it, and Bobby curled up and went to sleep.

Ed drove on for Dunes City, a tiny coastal village, and within a few miles he dropped off to sleep. The truck veered off the highway and onto the beach. Both men suddenly woke, and before anything could be done the truck rolled over on its top. The racks on the truck bed anchored in the sand and stopped the truck as it slid into the water. The hood sank six inches in the sand, while the top of the truck was smashed down and both windows were broken.

As the truck rolled over, the tools behind the seat fell and landed on the two men. A monkey wrench hit Ed in the head and knocked him cold. Bobby had screwdrivers, pliers, wrenches, a ballpeen hammer, and all sorts of nuts and bolts scattered on him.

The horses were tied in and upside down, kicking and fighting to break free. One near the tailgate shattered it with two solid kicks. Five head broke loose and escaped. Whirlwind, the big double rank mare, wasn't one of them. The loose horses loped straight into the sea just as a huge wave rolled in and were never seen again.

The force of the water rocked the truck, flooding water through the broken windows of the cab, then receded.

Bobby managed to squeeze out of his window, waded around to get Ed out and did, but pulled him right out of his boots in the process. About that time, a truckload of loggers came along.

They hooked a cable onto the truck and rolled it upright. Amazingly, Bobby, Ed, and all of the six horses left were uninjured.

The loggers stayed to help get the old truck started, and Bobby drove it the remaining thirty miles to Reedsport with caved-in top, broken windshield, shattered windows and all.

After they unloaded the broncs, they turned around and drove the truck back to the ranch in the same condition to get another load of horses.

Whirlwind peed all over when she bucked. She was the best saddle bronc they owned for four years, before she coliced and died. She might have been one of the greatest bucking horses of all time, had she lived.

The Christensen Brothers would only ever have a few saddle broncs in her class. War Paint and Miss Klamath were two.

10

The Girl from Alberta

Two years later, in 1931, the committee decided to add steer riding and calf roping to the upcoming rodeo at Crawfordsville. Bull riding wasn't introduced until later on in the thirties. But the steers back then weren't little light steers like they are today. They were big, teshy Corrientis crossed with swamp Brahmas out of Florida. Hank and Bobby bought a few more wet cows with calves to rope and some big steers for the steer riding.

One evening Hank and Bobby were heading home after doctoring one of their cows. Seeing a Model A Ford pickup truck coming up the road, they stopped their horses and watched the pickup until it stopped at the corrals.

"I wonder who that is?" Hank asked.

Hank and Bobby kicked their horses into a lope and pulled up when they reached the corral. The man opened the gate. When they were in the corral, he told them his name, Harvey Ward, and said he was looking for work.

Hank nodded and unsaddled.

"I was wondering if you need some help," Harvey said.

"You'll have to talk to my dad," Hank answered. "What can you do?"

He said he was a good hand with a horse, knew cattle, and had herded sheep a little.

At the house, Lawrence was taking a nap and Mollie had made some iced tea. She poured Harvey a glass and Hank and Bobby poured their own. She fixed lunch and asked Bobby to wake Lawrence up to eat. He ended up hiring Harvey and would work him until the spring of '35. Harvey helped them drive the horses and steers to Crawfordsville for the Fourth of July rodeo that year and told them he was quitting to get a job at the feed store in town.

The committee had voted to give the Christensens $500 to put on the rodeos from then until in the forties. They had built bleachers and six bucking chutes, as well as a chute for the timed events, and added bulldogging and tie-down team roping. Hank and Bobby had picked up a few more bucking horses and big steers for the steer riding and some lighter ones to rope and bulldog.

This would be their sixth year of furnishing the stock at Crawfordsville, and they had gotten to know a lot of the town folks. They also met quite a few girls and danced with most of them at the rodeo dances over those years, but hadn't gotten serious over any of them.

Gene Tyler was picking up for Bobby while he rode at the rodeo that year. He was the last bronc rider on Sunday afternoon and won it. After Gene had picked him up, a girl by the name of Eness Smith yelled at him. She was standing at the fence with another girl Bobby had never seen— a real pretty girl with long, dark hair.

"I seen you at the dance last night, did you see me?" Eness asked.

Bobby told her he had, but that he was too busy talking to Hank when he did and never got a chance to dance with her.

As Bobby got his chaps unbuckled, Eness told him she liked his ride and introduced him to the other girl.

"This is Lucille, my best friend."

It was obvious that Bobby wanted to meet her. He was surprised when Lucille told him she was Harvey Ward's sister.

Bobby had turned twenty-two the month before Lucille was twenty. She was from Alberta, Canada, and had five brothers besides Harvey. Her father had pulled out when he and her mother divorced, leaving her mother with six boys and Lucille in the sod house where Lucille was born. They lived there for three years before moving down to Sisters, Oregon, where Lucille grew up. They moved to Crawfordsville just before Harvey went to work at the ranch.

Bobby and Lucille began dating, and Bobby soon asked Lucille to marry him. They married in Eugene that winter and moved into a little house on the ranch. She fixed it up so that any man would be proud to live in it. She was a good cook and kept the house spotless, just as Bobby's mother had done.

The brothers drove the stock to Crawfordsville for ten years in a row to put on the rodeo before they bought a truck bigger than the bobtail.

Some pretty waspy hands came there in those early years: Paddy Ryan, Jessie Stahl, Earl Thode, Perry Henderson, Everett Bowman, Turk Greenough, Chuck Shepherd, Bill Linderman, Tom Bride, Gene Miles, Manuel Enos, Bill Hancock, Jim Eagan, Dick Murray, Bill Kunkle, and Bill Markley. Most all of them rode, roped, and bulldogged.

11

Wimpy the Sheep Dog

One day while Hank and Bobby were branding a bull, Lawrence was unharnessing his team and called them over to him.

"What do you boys think about us goin' in the sheep business? I hear they're sellin' for fifty cents a head in Portland."

Neither Hank nor Bobby was real fond of sheep, but neither made a comment. Hank shrugged his shoulders.

Lawrence informed the boys that there were more ways to make money with sheep than with cattle.

"It's your outfit, Pop," Hank said.

Lawrence folded his arms on his chest and responded. "Now, son, this is as much you kids' ranch as it is your mother's and mine. If you boys don't wanna fool with sheep, we won't!"

"I guess we can try a few," Hank said, and Bobby nodded his head.

"Okay," Lawrence smiled. "We'll drive up to the sale in Portland in the mornin' and see what they got."

They bought fifty head of ewes and one buck at the sale. There was good grass in the pasture where they turned them out when they were back home. Not even Lawrence knew much about sheep. A neighbor who had sheep told Lawrence there are tight wool sheep and loose wool sheep, and grass seed would get in tight wool sheep when they grazed. The wool would grow grass, but it would come right off with the wool when they sheared. On the other hand, the grass seed would simply fall out of the loose wool.

They attempted to shear by hand but were not very good at it. So they rigged a hand grinding stone to generate electricity and sheared with electric shears. After the lamb crop had matured, they bred the loose wool bucks to the tight wool ewes and eventually had all loose wool sheep.

Their first rodeo, after those early Crawfordsville rodeos, was at Oakdale, California, in 1940. They had bought more stock and needed some way to haul it to a big rodeo like that. Hank bought the old bobtail Dodge he had borrowed previously. It took six trips, driving day and night, with the brothers trading off the driving chore every hundred miles, to haul the stock to Oakdale.

On the last trip they were a few miles out of Oakdale when two mounted cowboys, Ben Johnson and his teenage son, Ben, Jr., started moving a herd of steers across the highway with two Border Collies. There must have been two hundred head in the bunch. Hank was driving and had to stop to wait for them to cross. They waved, and Bobby rolled down his window to wave back.

Ben, Sr. told the dogs to split the herd. One dog slipped into the part of the herd on the highway and drove them on across. The other dog held the rest from getting on the highway as Hank drove on.

Ben Johnson and Ben, Jr. showed up to rope at Oakdale. After they roped, Bobby and Ben, Jr. discussed the value of dogs in handling livestock. Bobby told Ben, Jr. he would sure like to have a dog like one of their Border Collies. Ben, Jr. said he had a bitch that had just weaned a litter of pups, and the next day he brought a male to Bobby. Bobby named the pup Wimpy.

The Johnsons moved to Oklahoma not long after that and bought a ranch. Ben, Jr. became the 1953 World Champion team roper. He later became a movie star and won an Academy Award in 1972 for his role in *The Last Picture Show*.

Clint Hall, a middle-aged cowboy who worked at the ranch, had a crush on Babe, but Mollie put a stop to that. She thought Clint was too old for Babe. Bill Markley, a steer wrestler and clown for Bobby and Hank, worked on the ranch when they weren't on the rodeo trail. He and Babe became acquainted and began dating. Eventually they married and moved into a little house on the ranch.

The women on the ranch fell in love with the cute little puppy named Wimpy. He was partial to Mollie and claimed a spot on her back porch. She was seldom seen without him at her side. Wimpy was totally loyal to her and quickly learned good manners and all kinds of chores. She taught him to go after Lawrence with a note tied around his neck when she wanted him to come to dinner.

Most of that year, Hank, Bobby, and Bill were on the road. When they came home in the slack season, Wimpy had grown quite a bit. Bobby tried to teach him to work sheep, but he would have no part of it. He'd just stand there and look at them. When Mollie was around, he would dash to her side.

One afternoon they were working the sheep in a set of portable corrals down where Bill and Babe lived. There were some big lambs in the bunch that were getting their tails bobbed. Wimpy was in the corral with the other dogs that day and, like him, none of the other dogs would work. They were worthless around sheep. All they would do was stand around and bark. Wimpy wouldn't even bark. He was alert, but he just sat there, watching.

All of a sudden one of the big lambs jumped a corral panel and took out across the field. Wimpy's ears shot up. He began barking at the fleeing lamb and lunged to a panel in the fence, scrambled under it, tore out in a wide circle, got around the lamb, drove him back to the corral and inside the gate.

That was all it took for Wimpy to know that his purpose in life was to be a stock dog. Mollie knew all along that a dog with his alertness and speed had to be a great stock dog.

Bobby took the job of training Wimpy. In no time, all he had to do was tell the dog what he wanted and Wimpy would do it. When they were trying to cut a certain one out of a herd of sheep, all Bobby had to do was point at it and sic Wimpy. Wimpy would stretch out until his belly was barely off the ground, sneak most vigilantly through the herd, catch the one he wanted gently by the nape of the neck, and quietly bring him out of the bunch. He was an amazing dog.

In a couple of months the Christensens leased a thousand acres on the Rice ranch up by Roseburg to run a thousand head of sheep on. The lease was fenced on three sides and ran to the coast. The ocean was the back fence. The sheep had to be checked as often as possible. When Bobby had the chance he would load a horse, whistle Wimpy up, and they would head to the Rice lease.

One fall day Bobby unloaded his horse at the top end of the pasture on the Rice. The sheep stayed on top. There was feed all over the pasture, but sheep don't travel far like cattle when they graze.

When Bobby found the herd there were approximately a hundred head gone. Their tracks led due west, heading toward the backside.

As Bobby sat on his horse, meditating on what route to take, Wimpy smelled a spot in the grass, looked up at Bobby, pointed his ears south and tore away in the very direction the sheep had gone. Bobby eased his horse over to the spot Wimpy had smelled and saw a bear track.

He pulled his .30-30 from the holster under his leg, levered a shell in the chamber, and struck a lope south. He didn't have to go far before he saw Wimpy sitting in the trail ahead, calmly looking up a little fir tree. Bobby stopped his horse, knowing the dog had something treed.

Bobby eased his pony close enough to see a cub climbing out

on a branch of the tree. Then breaking brush began to echo from the timber somewhere close. Bobby knew it was the old mama bear coming. He knew she was on the fight the way she was crashing through the brush. Bobby squalled at Wimpy and spurred his horse the hell out of there. He was quite a way down the trail before he pulled up. Wimpy was not to be seen anywhere. There was a good chance mama bear had killed the dog.

Bobby's horse started dancing sideways, and here comes Wimpy fogging down the trail, heading straight toward Bobby with all he had. The big, black mama bear was right on top of him. Wimpy never backed off when he passed Bobby's horse. The horse reared, fighting to get away from Bobby's control, when the bear slammed on the brakes, drove her butt in the ground, and slid to a stop right in front of the horse. The horse broke in two and bucked Bobby off. When he had his eyes back in focus, he saw his horse turning the crank down the trail and mama bear making tracks up the trail.

After Bobby ran down his horse and swung on, he never caught sight of Wimpy again until he hit an old logging road about a half mile down. Wimpy was sitting in the road, as big as you please. Bobby stepped off his horse and rested with Wimpy for a minute or two, then headed on south the way the sheep had gone.

A few miles passed before they were on a long ridge. By standing in his stirrups, Bobby could see over a little rise. He moved his eyes along until they found the sheep grazing in a bunch not far from the coast. Five or six were down. Bobby knew they were dead.

It was obvious that something had cut them off from the big herd back up the country and drove them down to where they were. It was doubtful the mama bear had done it. Female bears seldom wrangle that many sheep out of a big herd. More than likely, a boar had done it. Boars are notorious for gathering up a little bunch in the fall of the year and pushing them off someplace. They will kill a few during the warm months, eat what they want, and leave the rest to rot. When the weather began to turn cold, they would kill a few more and fill up with all the mutton they could eat and hibernate all winter.

Wimpy was standing beside the horse. Bobby slapped his leg, and the dog jumped up in the saddle in front of him. He pointed out the sheep to Wimpy and told him to bring them. Wimpy jumped to the ground and sailed out. It wasn't long before Wimpy was back with the sheep. It took him about a half-hour to get them there, but he did.

Although he had never been in that piece of country before, Wimpy took the whole herd back to the ranch as though he had been that way a hundred times.

Bobby knew he'd need help destroying the menacing bear and contacted a government trapper and four or five guys with good dogs. The bear had slaughtered every dog but Wimpy by the time they found him. Wimpy was too quick for the bear and kept him at bay until the men killed him.

12

The Pony Express

By 1941 most of the stock contractors, including the Christensen Brothers, were using bulls. A big Brahma they named Sleepy was the first bull they bought. By the time the sale ended, they had bought nine more head.

When they secured the contract for Livermore that year, they discovered they had two crippled bulls. Consequently, they needed more and began shaving the country to find them and did so. All the bulls bucked at Livermore, and only five were ridden in two days. Ol' Sleepy wasn't one of them.

Hank got on the road after Livermore and started getting contracts all over California and Oregon. They rolled the rest of that summer.

That fall Roy Craft come out to the ranch, bearing news that some guy from New York was claiming nobody could run a pony express race faster than some boys did back east.

"He'll challenge anybody in this part of the country," Craft stated. "He says he'll bet five hundred dollars. So I bet him that you boys could."

"Did you put up the money already?" Hank asked.

Craft nodded his head. "Yep! There's nobody around here I know that has seven faster horses than you fellas."

Neither Hank nor Bobby was the kind to brag, but they knew they had seven horses that might work.

"How far does this New York guy want us to run?" Hank asked.

"Seventy-five miles from Eugene to Salem," Craft replied.

Hank looked at Bobby. "What do you think?"

Bobby nodded and told Craft to set the date. The men backing the race had already decided on the following Saturday.

The next day Hank and Bobby saddled two horses and headed up the highway toward Salem to map out a trail. There was a little wagon road that ran along the highway. They chose that to be the best route. Every ten miles they tied a rag in a tree or bush so they would know where to tie each relay horse.

Hours ahead of the starting time on the morning of the race, they loaded nine head of horses in the bobtail and hauled them to the spots where they had tied each rag. Bobby would start on the outskirts of Eugene, and Hank drove to his first relay horse forty miles away.

A local businessman fired the starting shot. Bobby laid the whip to his horse, a leggy bay gelding. He lunged with a burst of speed, penned his ears, and smoked the dust off the wagon road until he reached his first change horse, tied to a tree. Bobby bailed off on the fly, jerked the change horse's reins loose, and vaulted into the saddle. He kept that up to run the first half.

Hank swung up on the next horse, whipping and spurring to his next horse and so on.

The State Capitol building was the finish line. A big crowd, standing behind the governor of Oregon, was waiting when Hank got there. One of the governor's aides had a stopwatch. The Christensen Brothers beat the New York boys by twenty minutes. Hank rode his horse up the steps and shook hands with the governor.

It turned out to be a lot bigger deal than Hank or Bobby thought it would. Roy Craft wasn't the only one who had bet on the race, and the Christensen name made headlines throughout Oregon and northern California.

13

Lynx Hollow

By this time the family was deep in the livestock business. Besides their rodeo stock, they had over a thousand head of sheep and two hundred mama cows and calves.

"I guess we're gonna have to build a new barn," Lawrence said one day when Hank and Bobby came down the ladder after patching a hole in the roof. "I reckon with you boys gone with your rodeos so much, we'll have to hire it done. Old man Mullens might just be our man."

"Mr. Mullens is older than you, Pop," Hank said. "He couldn't get around good enough to build a barn."

"Sure, he's too old," Lawrence retorted. "He'd have to hire a man or two to help 'em, but there's plenty of big, strappin' younguns around Eugene that kin swing a hammer."

Old man Mullens lived a mile or two beyond the ranch. He had come there from Nebraska or Iowa, or someplace in the Midwest, a few years earlier. Mullens was truly handy. He could do about anything when it came to building or farming and had a lot of savvy about many other things, too.

"I'll tell ya what, ma'am. You get your old man ta give me

some ground," Mr. Mullens had said to Mollie, "and I'll grow ya as good a crop as you'll ever see."

Lawrence gave him five acres and a team of horses with a cultivator, and he grew a good stand of corn.

Old man Mullens and his little wife came by the house to visit a day or so after Hank and Bobby had patched the barn roof, and Lawrence brought up the subject of building the barn

"All I need's the dad-burn lumber," Mr. Mullens said. "Don't need no nails, nary a one. I use wood pegs. But ya got ta let me have all the time I need. Don't never work fast, ya understand? I don't need no help neither! Just a might bit a shade ta rest under and the use of a tall ladder and a good stout horse."

Lawrence laid out the foundation, and every day the old man plugged along by himself. A year later he had a new barn built. There were seven stalls in the barn: five for saddle horses, one to milk in, and one to sheer sheep in (twice as big as the other six).

They had a hundred acres in alfalfa hay. The hayloft was big enough to hold twenty tons, but that was far from enough to last through a tough winter. There was an old barn near the house where Hank lived. It was smaller than the new barn and would only hold ten tons, but at least it was extra storage.

The ranch was close enough to the coast that the snow was seldom too deep for the stock to graze. So with what grass they could feed on and a supplement of hay, the livestock stayed fat all winter.

Hank and Bobby had built up their rodeo string considerably from what they had started with. They had an ample supply of roping stock and bulldogging steers, around a hundred head of bucking horses and over fifty head of bulls, plus the cattle and sheep. In time they began to run out of summer pasture.

Lawrence knew a man by the name of Huff who had 1,200 acres for sale on Lynx Hollow, quite a way up the country from them. He had run a logging outfit there years before. Lawrence had logged it off for him, and there hadn't been anything grazing on it for years except wild game. The grass was stirrup deep, and there was plenty of water.

Huff offered it to Lawrence for five dollars an acre, and he bought it. Like the Rice place, the bottom end wasn't fenced and ran to the Pacific Coast. This was government land but it wasn't under lease by anyone and had no stock on it. It ran for a good thirty miles beyond the Huff place, giving the Christensens access to thousands of acres of open country.

With the bottom unfenced, the cattle could go anywhere they took a notion. That could create a problem, but the Christensens would wait until it came up before they would worry about it.

Huff had built a good house and a set of corrals just down the canyon from where the logging camp had been. It was a perfect place for a cowboy to live and keep track of the herd, but they didn't have enough help to keep a man there. Lawrence thought about hiring someone, but one man couldn't have kept the cattle from straying, not without riding the bottom in a lope day and night. And they didn't have time to fence that end, making things even more difficult.

Then Lawrence came up with an idea.

"I'll tell you what, boys," he said when they were discussing the problem. "We'll bell a hundred cows and see what happens. I know they'll have the freedom to stray plum to the coast, but with the bells on 'em we can gather 'em easy enough."

Even if the ranch was a family outfit, Hank and Bobby respected any suggestions Lawrence or Mollie made. So as crazy as they thought the idea was, they kept it to themselves.

Hank and Bobby had to spend a whole afternoon heading and heeling the cows to put the bells on. They didn't have a squeeze chute.

Besides Hank and Bobby, Babe and Bill Markley and a hired hand, Bill Kunkle, would help on the drive. Both Bills were as handy as a chap pocket at anything they did.

It was just past sunup and they were ready to start up the country with the herd when Manuel Enos came up, driving an old rattly car. The dust boiling up behind the car looked like an Oklahoma twister. Manuel was one of the toughest All-Around cowboys in Oregon. He worked the bronc riding and bareback riding and had never been bucked off a bareback horse. He was also a good cowboy in the brush. And there were few men in that country who could whip him in a fistfight.

When he got out of the car he trotted up to the corral with his chaps a'flopping and his spurs strapped on his boots. "Mornin', boys! Sorry I held you fellas up. Oops, you too, Babe. I had a cute little skirt that wouldn't turn loose of me 'til it went to breakin' light. What horse you want me to ride?"

Hank told him to catch a little snip-nosed bay horse called Snip. It didn't take him but a jiffy to stack his outfit on Snip after he roped him. Bill Kunkle got off his horse and opened the gate for Manuel about the time he threw a leg over his saddle.

Snip was a little ouchy to get on and would buck if untracked too quickly, especially early in the morning. But that's exactly what Manuel did. Snip bogged his head, kicked off the lid, and bucked out the gate. Before Bill could get the gate shut, the loose horses in the corral stampeded out behind Snip and left the scene in a dead run.

Snip was tearing up the country, with Manuel hanging and rattling and grabbing anything he could to keep from taking wing. He was desperately trying to get his foot in his flopping outside stirrup and stay aboard Snip at the same time.

The stampeding remuda was about to jump Live Creek. It was a horse race for a mile before they got around them and drove them to the horse pasture, then headed for the high country.

The drive was slow and hot. They were all tuckered out by the time they reached the old house Huff had built. They threw the cattle in the corral and left Bill Kunkle there to feed them for a week before they were turned out. Everything was branded, so they didn't have to worry about that. If Lawrence's idea about putting bells on a hundred of the cows worked, the deal would run as smooth as silk.

And it did.

The Christensen boys were rodeoing pretty hard. Hank was

steer wrestling and was the arena director everywhere they went. Bobby was driving one of the trucks and picking up broncs. Bill Markley started clowning and steer wrestling, while Bill Kunkle drove the other truck and rode broncs.

There was little time left to check on cows as much as they would have liked to. They were only able to look them over about once a month, when one of them had time to ride through the herd. Every time, they found the cattle fat and slick, grazing and licking their calves. It was a surprise that the cattle never strayed off the 1,200 acres.

14

One Life Taken, One Life Given

After the Japanese hit Pearl Harbor in 1941, Uncle Sam wasted no time drafting Hank. But he failed his physical for having flat feet. A nineteen-year-old cousin, Jack Almasie, was helping them hay at the ranch. When the war broke out, he joined the navy.

Because Bill Markley was running the lower end of the ranch and beef was so extremely important to the war effort, he was deferred from the draft. Clint Hall had come to work on the ranch before the war and joined the navy. He returned to work at the ranch when the war ended.

Lucille and Bobby had their first child, Bobby, Jr., on January 20, 1945. Two weeks later, Lawrence died. People from all over that end of Oregon attended the funeral. Many cowboys wore sunglasses during the service. The reason was obvious: "Cowboys ain't supposed to cry."

If anything could have soothed Bobby and Lucille's grief after losing Lawrence, it was the birth of Bobby Lawrence Christensen, to be called Bobby, Jr. Not all the money in the world could have done more for either. He was a hardy baby and as healthy as a newborn colt.

Bobby knew the army would be calling him in any day. He

did receive draft papers to report to Camp Pendleton, but fortunately the war was over by then and he didn't have to go.

Jack Almasie never returned. He was on the USS *Houston,* an aircraft carrier, when a Japanese suicide plane dove down and sank it.

When news of the end of the war came, the whole country went crazy. A wild conglomeration of people was gathered at the depot in Eugene. Short, tall, fat and skinny people. Store clerks, businessmen, ranchers, and farmers. Ecstatic wives and sweethearts, budding girls, nervous mothers, and smiling old ladies. Gangly boys, old men, and broken-down cowboys. Indian, Mexican, Norwegian, Swedish, Italian, Jew and Gentile alike.

Everyone was watching a cloud of gray smoke funneling from the troop train's big engine and trailing above a long coupling of troop cars hooked to it. The cheering crowd muffled the shrill whistle when the train came in sight.

Clouds of steam hissed and spewed from the drivers as the heavy engine clattered past the crowd. The engineer was waving out his window and blowing his whistle in short yanks. Troops from every branch of the service were hanging out their windows. The train clamored to a stop. With duffel bags hoisted, soldiers, sailors, marines, paratroopers, and a few pretty WACS and WAVES began unloading. Everyone in the whole world seemed to be there—laughing, crying, cheering, hugging, kissing, and standing under a fog of confetti and balloons so thick that a flock of geese couldn't have flown through it. Rainbows of paper streamers rippled above tiny, waving American flags. Men sailed their hats into the air. And in the background was a long line of honking cars parked in the streets and a stampede of unbridled children chasing free-spirited balloons. The children were running, laughing, yelling, sliding down shiny car fenders, and crawling over narrow hoods.

Relatives burst from the crowd and into the open arms of the war heroes. Majorettes, tossing spiraling batons, led thundering drums, crashing cymbals, and blaring horns down the crowded streets while jazz bands played the jitterbug.

By the time the war ended, Bobby, Jr. wasn't just walking—he was riding a horse. Bobby found a little half-Quarter horse, half-Welsh pony named Lucky and bought him for Bobby, Jr. when he was three years old. Soon he was a good enough little hand to help drive the drags when they moved cattle. And old Lucky was a pretty good cow-horse for as little as he was. If a man was riding point, he could see nothing but Bobby, Jr.'s hat behind the herd.

Lucky proved his worth during hunting season as well, because if you didn't hunt deer you didn't run with the Christensens. They lived on deer meat. Fourteen freezers on the ranch were kept full of venison the year round. The cattle and sheep went to the sale every fall.

When Bobby, Jr. was nine they leased the old Barney Grub ranch up by Roseburg, along with quite a few other ranches. The deer on the other ranches weren't near as plentiful as on the Barney Grub, though it was on the Barney Grub that Bobby, Jr. shot his first buck at the age of nine. It was early one morning and as quiet as a funeral. Bobby and Bobby, Jr. were drifting across a big open meadow on horseback. Bobby, Jr. was on Lucky, bobbing along behind his dad. The only sounds were birds chirping, the tall grass dragging along Lucky's belly, and a little creek splashing over the rocks.

The ranch was thick with oak trees and brush and long on good grass. There were almost as many deer there as there were oak leaves. They stayed fat and as slick as seals on acorns. The nuts were an inch deep where they had fallen from the trees.

Bobby's horse stopped and threw up his ears. He was looking at four or five does standing in a little oak grove fifty or so yards away. Bobby looked back at his son and pointed them out.

Bobby, Jr. eased off of Lucky and laid the barrel of his .30-30 across his saddle.

"Them's all does, son," Bobby said.

"One's a buck, Dad," Bobby, Jr. corrected.

Bobby thought the lad had buck fever until he saw a three-point lying behind a dead log a few yards from the does. Bobby winked at Bobby, Jr., who grinned back, levered a shell in his rifle, squeezed one off, hit the buck square in the eye with one shot, and dropped him.

That did it. Bobby couldn't shut Bobby, Jr. up about hunting for a week. After they had the buck gutted, slung over a horse, and were headed to the bobtail, Bobby, Jr. pestered his father about when they would go again all the way to the truck.

The ride back was a good fifteen miles. Breakfast was a long ways behind them and Bobby was plenty hungry. He knew Bobby, Jr. was too, but he never whined about it. He was a pretty tough kid and never whined about anything. By the time they reached the bobtail it was way past noon and dinner.

They were back to the home ranch in Eugene after dark. Lucille got out of bed and fed them supper. At breakfast the next morning, Bobby, Jr. was still excited about the deer he had killed. He burned his mother's ears with the details.

Lucille looked at Bobby when Bobby, Jr. finished his story and spoke. "Those deer that are ruining our apple orchard are what you boys need to shoot."

They had put in a new apple orchard that spring. A big buck had been slipping in at night, eating the young apples and pushing over the little trees that hadn't rooted well. He would sneak in about 2:00 or 3:00 in the morning when no one was awake. Bobby could tell it was a big buck by the size of his tracks.

That night he told Bobby, Jr. if he could get out of bed that early, he could see if he could get the deer. The lad got the buck with one shot.

15

Miss Klamath's Last Jump

In July 1954 the Christensens had the contract for the five-day rodeo in Ogden, Utah.

Lucille, expecting her second child, was busy packing things for the trip to Ogden, five days away. Bobby, Jr. was in the front room, listening to the radio, when Lucille came in the room. "You better go to bed, honey," she said. "Dad wants to get an early start in the morning."

They had to leave the following morning to allow the stock a three-day rest.

Bobby, Jr. was up and dressed with his parents at 3:00 A.M., ready to help load the broncs, two pickup horses, and a horse for the judge to flag on. It was still dark when Lucille joined the men at the pens. Bobby told the truck drivers he would have motel rooms waiting for them when they reached Ogden.

When Bobby, Lucille, and Bobby, Jr. rolled into Ogden, Bobby, Jr. was starving. They ate supper after they settled in the motel. The stock trucks, with drivers Manuel Enos, Gene Miles, and Bill Kunkle, didn't arrive in Ogden until the following morning.

Miss Klamath, the best saddle bronc they had, was scheduled to go in the first round at Ogden. More than likely, whoever had her drawn figured he had no chance of riding the waspy old bronc and didn't show up.

Manuel Enos volunteered to mount her out and ride her exhibition. There wasn't a ranker horse alive at that time—perhaps there never will be. Odds are that there are only a couple of bronc riders alive today who could make the whistle on her.

The Christensen Brothers had bought the big, feather-legged bay mare from Spooky Bishop, a rancher from near Brothers, Oregon, when she was a ten-year-old. She had come out of a band of mustangs that ran in the high desert country around Brothers and Burns. Spooky ran wild horses with his son and told the Christensens they'd trapped the big, raw-boned, broomtail mustang.

Not to take anything away from Bill Ward; he was one of the toughest saddle bronc riders in the world at that time. But if the big mare hadn't hit the fence at the Klamath Falls rodeo, there are many old-time bronc riders still around who don't believe he would have ridden her. The emblem on the PRCA's logo is taken from a picture of Bill Ward at San Antonio, Texas, in those early years.

Every bronc peeler in that part of the country had tried the long-headed rangy, common-looking mare. She flattened them all!

The Christensen Brothers tried out the big mare at Red Bluff, California, where Spooky had trailed her for them to look at. Manuel Enos tried her. When he had the heels of his boots pushed in the stirrups and lifted his rein against her neck, he nodded—and the big, rangy mare scattered him all over the arena. Needless to say, they bought her. They started to call her Miss Red Bluff, but decided on Miss Klamath.

War Paint, another of the Christensens' great horses, was a big, showy, good-looking brown and white spotted gelding. He was so well publicized in newspapers and magazines that no one could forget him. But he never bucked a jump better than Miss Klamath.

Although she was on the pro rodeo trail only a few short years, she rung out every tough buckin' horse rider that stepped across the seat of his bronc saddle.

There were fewer saddle bronc riders around back then—bronc riders with the seat of their britches made of world champion material, like the boys today. Peelers like Scott Johnson, Dan Mortensen, Ty Murray, Tom Reeves, Chance Dixon, Jessie Bail, Denny and Rod Hay, the Etbauer brothers, and so on.

Although the greats thirty and forty years ago were only a handful, their skill was honed and they rode as well as the top thirty do today. And Miss Klamath rung them all out. Toughs like Casey Tibbs, Deb Copenhaver, Guy Weeks, Marty Woods, Jim and Tom Tescher, Enoch Walker, Jackie Wright, and others.

They never gave awards for saddle broncs back then. For that matter, no awards were given for any bucking stock. The only award Miss Klamath ever wore was an ordinary old bronc halter. But if they would have named the bucking horse of the year when Miss Klamath was alive, there's no doubt she would have won the title five years on the rodeo trail.

The big mare stood quietly in the chute as usual while Manuel set his Hamley, snugged it down, and measured his rein. The measure was a fist behind the cantle. After Manuel slipped his rein under the halter, she stood looking out in the arena, twitching her ears and rolling her eyes. Manuel stood over her until the chute boss told him to pull his cinch. The bronc ahead jumped out and flattened the rider just before the whistle.

Miss Klamath remained quiet while Manuel took his rein from under the halter, checked it once more, eased in his saddle, and slipped his feet in his stirrups. Mel Lambert's voice came over the loudspeaker: "Manuel Enos will wind up today's saddle bronc riding on Miss Klamath. This great mare is fifteen years old and has bucked for five of those years. She has only been ridden one time; Bill Ward conquered her at Klamath Falls, Oregon. This is phenomenal for a saddle bronc, for any bucking animal for that matter. Although today is only an exhibition ride, it should prove to be a great contest between two great athletes."

Manuel nodded his head as Mel's words drifted to the clouds. Miss Klamath jumped out. She hit the ground with her knees locked and cracked her hocks over her head so hard it sounded like a shotgun blast. The rosin on Manuel's chaps squeaked, but he held his swell. The big mare practically threw her head back in his lap the second jump. Manuel stretched his arm as high as he could to hold the slack out of the rein. It did him no good. When Miss Klamath took her head back and cracked her hocks again, she ripped his swells away and blasted him ten feet in the air. When she came down, both back legs snapped like matchsticks, and she fell. The scene was pitiful as she courageously struggled to get up. But it was no use; she died.

The news of this spectacular mare's death grieved every cowboy. Everyone loved her, and there wasn't a dry eye when they drug the old campaigner out of the arena that gloomy night and buried her.

Ogden was back to back with Eugene. Hank was so distressed over the mare's death that he got good and drunk that night, trying to wash away his memories of her. Although the drunk did nothing for his grief, he had to shake it and jumped in his Cadillac to leave for Eugene as quickly as the last perf at Ogden ended.

Bobby got the stock loaded by 10:00 that Monday night. Then he, Lucille, and Bobby, Jr. headed out to make a flying trip back to Eugene. Lucille could go into labor at any time.

An early photo taken at the logging camp where Mollie met Lawrence (Mollie far left, back row; Lawrence far left, seated).

Early photo of Bob riding a cow on the home ranch.

Rex the Dog.

Early Rodeo CB Ranch, 1920s.

Branding at the CB.

Lawrence Christensen.

Henry with his bulldogging horse.

Mollie Christensen, Round-up Parade, Eugene, OR (circa 1940s).

Mollie Christensen, home ranch (circa 1962).

Bob and Lucille Christensen with Bobby, Jr., 1946.

Ranch riding.

New bulls, 1942.

Another new bull, 1942.
(Photo courtesy Myra Gordon)

Christensen Ranch in the early days.

Cy Taillon and Gene Payne, rodeo announcers, 1947, Puyallup, WA. (Photo courtesy Lee Merrill)

Jimmie Sloan on Rattler, Molalla, OR, 1944. (Photo by DeVere Helfrich from Donald C. and Elizabeth M. Dickinson Research Center, National Cowboy and Western Heritage Museum, Oklahoma)

Bill Markley on Calico Day, Portland, OR, 1943. (Photo by DeVere Helfrich from Donald C. and Elizabeth M. Dickinson Research Center, National Cowboy and Western Heritage Museum, Oklahoma)

Larry Daniels on Orphan Annie, Roseburg, 1948. (Photo by DeVere Helfrich from Donald C. and Elizabeth M. Dickinson Research Center, National Cowboy and Western Heritage Museum, Oklahoma City, OK)

Eddie Akridge, steer wrestling, Crawfordsville, 1948. (Photo by DeVere Helfrich from Donald C. and Elizabeth M. Dickinson Research Center, National Cowboy and Western Heritage Museum, Oklahoma City, OK)

Eddie Akridge on Northwestern, Roseburg, 1948. (Photo by DeVere Helfrich from Donald C. and Elizabeth M. Dickinson Research Center, National Cowboy and Western Heritage Museum, Oklahoma City, OK)

Sonny Tureman on Treasure Island, Ellensburg Round Up, 1948.

Stub Bartlemay on Little Boyce, Medford, Oregon, 1948. (Photo by DeVere Helfrich from Donald C. and Elizabeth M. Dickinson Research Center, National Cowboy and Western Heritage Museum, Oklahoma City, OK)

Gene Miles on Northwestern, Cottage Grove, 1950. (Photo by DeVere Helfrich from Donald C. and Elizabeth M. Dickinson Research Center, National Cowboy and Western Heritage Museum, Oklahoma City, OK)

Howard Allen holding on as he leaves Mighty Mouse, Eureka, California, 1950. (Photo by DeVere Helfrich from Donald C. and Elizabeth M. Dickinson Research Center, National Cowboy and Western Heritage Museum, Oklahoma City, OK)

Bob Christensen on John Day, Portland, OR. (Photo by DeVere Helfrich from Donald C. and Elizabeth M. Dickinson Research Center, National Cowboy and Western Heritage Museum, Oklahoma City, OK)

Ben Johnson (1953 Champion) heading, Oliver Sims heeling. (Photo by DeVere Helfrich from Donald C. and Elizabeth M. Dickinson Research Center, National Cowboy and Western Heritage Museum, Oklahoma City, OK)

CB Rodeo crossing Columbia on ferry.

Cow Palace—Christensen Brothers Show Champions. Left to right: Ross Dallarhide, All-Around, Vern Castro, John Bowman, Gordon Davis, calf roping, Jack Hara, Jack Spurling, Sonny Tureman. Front row: Bobby Christensen, Sandy Dallarhide, Hank Christensen. 1953. (Geo. W. Baker)

Eddie Akridge and Sonny Tureman arrive in the Northwest for a CB Rodeo, circa 1950.

1954 CB Rodeo champions. Henry second from left, Bob second from right. (Frank Olson)

Casey Tibbs off Miss Klamath, 1954. (Photo by DeVere Helfrich from Donald C. and Elizabeth M. Dickinson Research Center, National Cowboy and Western Heritage Museum, Oklahoma City, OK)

Miss Klamath cartoon from *Rodeo Sports News*, 1954. (Dixon)

Deb Copenhaver on Miss Klamath, Ellensburg, WA, 1952. (Photo by DeVere Helfrich from Donald C. and Elizabeth M. Dickinson Research Center, National Cowboy and Western Heritage Museum, Oklahoma City, OK)

The Christensen Brothers, Hank, left, and Bob, Sr., circa 1959.

Western Washington Fair—rodeo announcer Cy Taillon visits with Slim Pickens and Bill Markley.

Bob, Sr. and Stub Johnson from St. Helens, OR.

Bob and Henry Christensen. (Lee Merrill)

Western Washington Fair Champions, circa 1950. (Lee Merrill photo for Western Washington Fair)

Bob and Hank Christensen present Casey Tibbs All-Around Award, 1954.

Hank and Bob Christensen. (Ben Allen-Rodeo Photos)

Bob and Hank Christensen, advertisement program.

Cartoon from 1956 *Rodeo Sports News*, notice CB brand on bull. (Pete Dixon)

Bert Frances off Tarzan.

Lebanon, OR, rodeo—Dean Oliver calf roping, 1958.

Greg Whalen on Loni Sanora 27.

Henry Christensen bulldogging.
(Ray Brogan)

Slim Pickens

Bob Christensen, Sr., 1962.

Mollie Christensen and Rex Allen.
(*Eugene Register* staff photo by Paul Petersen)

Bob picking up Mighty Mouse.

Eddie Akridge in Eugene, OR.

Christensen Brothers' Half Breed bucking off five-time World Champion Casey Tibbs, 1964. (Ben Allen-Rodeo Photos)

Billy Wilcoxson (author) on a Clear Day, bareback riding in Denver, 1965. (Photo by DeVere Helfrich from Donald C. and Elizabeth M. Dickinson Research Center, National Cowboy and Western Heritage Museum, Oklahoma City, OK)

Paul Mayo off High Society (CB), 8thGo NFR, Oklahoma City, 1965. (Photo by DeVere Helfrich from Donald C. and Elizabeth M. Dickinson Research Center, National Cowboy and Western Heritage Museum, Oklahoma City, OK)

Bill Stanton off #211, Porterville, 1966. (Ben Allen-Rodeo Photos)

Bob Wegner, 1962 World Champion, rides Snuffy—CB NFR bull (Pendleton Roundup).

Kenny McLean on Quick Silver, Pendleton, OR, 1964.

Harley May leaving CB's Quick Silver, Ellensburg, WA, 1964.

Sniper,
CB NFR horse.
(Pasadena photo)

Bull throwing cowboy.

Jim Griggs on Pretty Boy (CB) at Red Bluff, 1966. (Photo by DeVere Helfrich from Donald C. and Elizabeth M. Dickinson Research Center, National Cowboy and Western Heritage Museum, Oklahoma City, OK)

A.K. Majors on Umpqua (CB) at Red Bluff, 1966. (Photo by DeVere Helfrich from Donald C. and Elizabeth M. Dickinson Research Center, National Cowboy and Western Heritage Museum, Oklahoma City, OK)

Bill Ward off War Paint and Manuel Enos on War Paint. (Photos by DeVere Helfrich from Donald C. and Elizabeth M. Dickinson Research Center, National Cowboy and Western Heritage Museum, Oklahoma City, OK)

Bob Christensen, Jr., riding Teachers Pet, Valley Springs, CA, 1968. (Al Fugell Studio)

Felix Cooper, Larry Mahan, and Bill Markley, Eugene, OR, 1968.

Shipping cattle at home ranch, 1966.

Wayne Harris on Smitty Clovis, California, 1978.

Bob Christensen and pen of bulls at the ranch.

Linda and Henry in Puyallup, Washington, 1953.
(Lee Merrill)

Vicki and Sherri feeding lambs, 1965. (Jim Vincent, *The Oregonian*)

Vicki Christensen and pony under ranch sign, 1962.
(Phil Wolcott, Jr., *Register-Guard*)

Sherri Christensen, Salinas, 1976. (Foxie Photo)

Vicki Christensen Felder, Salinas, 1976. (Foxie Photo)

Vicki Christensen trick riding, California Rodeo, Salinas, 1976. (Foxie Photo)

Kathy Christensen carrying flag at rodeo. (Photo by Lorena J. Blodget, Chico, California)

Bob Christensen and Harry Vold.

Linda Markholt, Oakdale, 1979. (Foxie Photo)

Bob Christensen, Jr., Jesse, and Bob, Sr., 1981.

Smith and Velvet, 1982 World Champion Bareback Horse.

Oscar's Velvet. (B. Allen)

Bob and Hank honored at Red Bluff Roundup, 1983. (B. Allen)

Bob and Rita Christensen, 1984.

Bob Christensen, Jr.

Bob Christensen hunting elk.

Bob Christensen, Jr. promotional photo. (F. Lyle)

The family gets together for the induction of Miss Klamath-Pro Rodeo Hall of Champions, Colorado Springs, CO, 1998. Back row, left to right: Jesse Christensen, Eddie Felder, Mel Parkhurst, Brett Tatum. Front row: Vicki Felder, Bob Sr., Linda Parkhurst, Bobby Christensen, Jr., Nancy Christensen, Anna Markholt, and Amy Markholt.

Jesse Christensen
(Photo by Phifer)

Brett Tatum, Woodlake 2000. (Eugene F. Hyder)

Jesse Christensen and cousin Brett Tatum behind the chutes.

Bob, Sr. and grandson Jesse, Norco, CA, 2002.
(Gene Hyder)

Bob Thain and Bob Christensen, Sr., Cowboy Hall of Fame Induction Ceremony.

Henry Christensen, Rodeo Man of the Year, 1982, Cowboy Hall of Fame, with wife Pat.

Bob Christensen, 1989 Induction, CB Pro Rodeo Hall of Fame. To Bob's right is Sherri Christensen accepting her dad Henry's plaque. Colorado Springs, Colorado.

Vicki Christensen Felder and her father, Bob Christensen, Sr., on his 90th birthday, June 2003.

Author Billy Wilcoxson (left) and Bob Christensen on Bob's 90th birthday.

16

Snowman and Iceman

It was August 14, 1954, the second day of the rodeo in Eugene. While Bobby was riding in the rodeo parade, Lucille was rushed to the Sacred Heart Hospital to have their baby.

Just as the parade passed Nemo's store, the owner ran out, pushed his way through the crowd, and yelled, "Hey, Bobby, you are the poppa of a new baby girl!"

Bobby would have spurred his horse all the way to the hospital to see his new daughter, but he was obligated to be at the rodeo to pick up broncs.

When the rodeo was over, he burned a pound of rubber off his Caddy to get to the hospital. He strutted down the hallway and entered Lucille's room with his spurs ringing on his boot heels, his hat in his hand, and lit up like 2001 Las Vegas when he saw Victoria Lynn Christensen lying in her mother's arms.

Mollie and Babe were there for Lucille for the first week after she and Vicki got home, but Bobby didn't get to see much of them. The rodeo business was going full bore.

One of the bulls got down and crippled in the truck coming

home after Klamath Falls. He wasn't one of their best bulls, just average. He bucked pretty good and threw off quite a few guys, but they couldn't afford to lose even one bull, not even an average one, so they started looking for one to replace him. Every farmer and rancher they talked to had a bull or two that might buck, but they weren't for sale.

It is a roll of the dice to speculate on the prospect of a horse or bull's ability to buck. Most any horse that isn't broke will buck a few times, but the ones that last are few and far between. The same with bulls. They can look like they would be rank son-of-a-bucks, but after they're ridden a few times they can go sour. Once in a while that kind will fight the clown and are worth keeping.

Bobby and Bobby, Jr. scoured the country with a fine-toothed comb until they finally found one. He had some age on him and they knew he wouldn't last, but they needed a bull bad and he was cheap, so they bought him.

"We need some young bulls," Hank told Bobby after he saw the bull.

"Maybe there'll be something at that breeders' sale in Eugene," Bobby said. "It's on a Wednesday the second week of next month. If we're lucky we'll be between rodeos."

Bill Markley went to the sale with Hank, Bobby, and Bobby, Jr. The sale was long and drawn out. Two or three bulls went through the ring with possibilities, but they were outbid. The bulls that did sell sold high—too high for untried bucking bulls.

When the Christensens were about to leave, twelve Charolais yearlings came in the ring. They were all snorty and muscled-up good. After the bids were started, Hank nodded to Bobby, indicating the quality of the young bulls. The guy in the ring thought he was bidding and called it.

If Hank were intending to bid he would have let a few more bids go to see how high the yearlings would get, but his nod bought the bulls.

It was after dark by the time they hauled the yearlings to the ranch. Mollie was having a big supper for everyone at her house, so the men decided they would haul the yearlings to the Huff place and put them with the cows the next morning.

"Did you get anything bought?" Mollie asked after the men washed up and sat down at the table.

"We got twelve nice yearlin's," Hank answered.

"How old do they have to be before they're big enough to buck?" Lucille asked.

"Three-year-olds, honey," Bobby answered.

"We should get some good buckin' bulls if we cross them with them whiteface cows," Hank said.

There was no disagreement about that, and the next morning they were up at first light. Gene Miles had the truck backed up to the loading chute. Bobby, Jr. wanted to drive them up. He would rather go horseback than in a truck anytime, but dads always make the final decisions and they took the bobtail.

Twenty-five or so cows were in sight when they reached the Huff place. There was an unloading chute at the corrals, but Bobby decided to jump the young bulls out in the pasture with the cows and located a good bank to back the bobtail against. Bobby, Jr. climbed the sideboards while his dad opened the tailgate. He admired his dad's strength as he watched him lift the heavy gate and set it aside. Bobby, Jr. was anxious to chouse the yearlings out.

The two alert enough to look out the back at the green freedom sniffed the air, lowered their heads, sniffed again, and bravely bailed out. The others scrambled, stumbled, clawed, and scratched their hooves on the slick floor and parachuted. No prodding necessary!

The first chance they had to check on the cattle, after putting the yearlings in with the cows, they discovered every yearling, except two, had high-tailed it and were scattered all the way to the coast.

When the two that stayed grew into three-year-olds, they were named Snowman and Iceman. The first time the Christensens bucked them was at Medford, Oregon. Snowman turned out to be the better of the two, but they both went to the

National Finals more than once. They were two of the best bucking bulls the Christensen Brothers ever owned.

Vicki grew and was walking and saying a few words in no time. Bobby, Jr. watched over her in a big brotherly manner, when he wasn't at a rodeo with his dad or at school.

17

Two for One

In the fall of '58, when the Christensen Brothers were a week from going to the Cow Palace, Hank told Bobby that Kenneth Paul "KP" Cooke, who had secretaried some of their early rodeos, had called. He said that Paul wanted to come to the ranch and go hunting with them. Bobby never turned down an invitation to hunt deer.

K. P. showed up early the next morning and had breakfast with them. After they topped off bacon and eggs and the last cup of coffee, Bobby whistled for Blackie, one of his dogs, while they headed for the pickup.

Bobby, Jr. had to go to school. He knew when he got home that afternoon he'd hear a good hunting story, but he never dreamed he'd hear one as unique as the one the men would bring home.

There were plenty of deer on the Eugene ranch; they didn't drive far, maybe fifteen miles, and they stopped at the end of the ranch where Bill and Babe lived on the river.

Babe brewed up a pot of coffee for the men to visit over about the cow business for twenty or thirty minutes. It wasn't far from there to reach a place deep in the mountains, where man and beast become one akin to the wild.

Soon they came to the fading ruts of a tired logging road leading past a few feeble cabins: remnants of carefully stacked logs rotting from years in the sharp claws of winter and the blazing fangs of summer; homes left by a past generation of misplaced souls who had known little in life except hardships and damn tough work.

Hank and Bobby knew of a secluded prune orchard tucked away in a little April meadow farther up the country. The soft, purple fruit kept the elk, deer, and bear prospering throughout the year.

It was midmorning when they reached the orchard, a little too late in the day for any game. When on the move, the deer and elk traveled certain trails. Hank and Bobby knew them all. The surrounding territory was straight up and straight down with deep hushed hollows, symbolic ravines, brushy gullies, and a legion of mighty, time-enduring fir and rigid, stable oak.

The radiator popped and grumbled as though it was trying to explode the water cap through the hood when Bobby switched off the pickup engine in the shade of the orchard. Snapping bolt and lever action rang through the mountain air as the men pumped shells in the chambers of their rifles and clicked on their safeties. Scopes and open sights were checked. A plan was mapped out on the ground, and the tough climb ahead began.

Hank left the trail and climbed the terrain, ascending to circle above the trail and drop back down to it around two miles ahead. Bobby and K. P. hoofed on to the switchbacks that crawled along the rim of a ravine gouged in the side of the mountain they were climbing. K. P. dropped down in the ravine when he found accessible footing. Bobby stayed on the trail. The plan was that there would be deer between them and Hank. With K. P. moving in the ravine below and Bobby moving up the trail, they would drive the deer to Hank.

In about an hour and a half Hank's first shot discharged. A minute or so later, Hank shot again. Then the air grew graveyard still. Suddenly, what sounded like a stampeding herd busting down the side of the mountain through the brush shattered the stillness. Two hundred yards in front of Bobby a big six-point bounced across the trail and turned up the country before he hit the gully where K. P. was. Bobby crouched to get a shot. The buck was going away from him and gaining ground. Bobby was using an open sight .30-30. He fired. Two big bucks crashed to the ground on their briskets. Leaping over the tangling brush, Blackie ran to them, barking the victory of the kill. Bobby scrambled behind Blackie. An enormous eight-point lay lifeless in the brush along with the six-point.

The bucks had been moving single file, so Bobby could only see the six-point. His bullet passed through it to find its final resting place in the eight-point.

Bobby was cutting the eight-point buck's throat when K. P. appeared. "I could swear I only heard one shot," he said.

Bobby looked up at K. P. and winked. "You did."

"Are you telling me you killed them both with one shot?" K. P. asked.

"They're both dead, aren't they?" Bobby answered.

Hank walked up and looked down at the two deer with a puzzled expression. "I didn't hear but one shot."

K. P. nodded as he took his skinning knife out. "Yeah, Daniel Boone here killed them both with one shot."

Bobby told his obedient dog to stay with the kill after they gutted and skinned the bucks. Blackie parked his rump near them and watched the three men head down the trail.

Bobby, Jr. was home from school when they got back to the ranch and told the story. He thought it was a sensational stroke of luck to get two deer with one shot, but the part about his father's deadly shot through the top of the six-point's neck was no surprise; the accuracy of shooting was in his genes.

After the men had coffee, Bobby and Bobby, Jr. saddled horses and, leading two to pack the deer, headed out. Blackie hadn't moved an inch from his post and jumped to his feet wagging at high speed when the two rode up.

Like his father, Bobby, Jr. was not big. But also like his father, at fourteen he was plenty damn stout. The eight-point weighed around 180 and the six-point a few pounds less. When they had them tied across the two packhorses, they swung up in their saddles and headed down the switchbacks. At the prune orchard they hit a trot for home. Blackie stayed in view, bouncing through the brush.

Not long after Bobby killed the two bucks with one shot, the ranch gained two new full-time employees. Gene Miles, one of Oregon's great saddle bronc riders, and Jack Halter had worked on the ranch, off and on, since before the war. During that time, the Christensen family had generously given them an acre apiece to build themselves homes. Gene was handy doing anything on the ranch, but mostly drove a truck and helped at the rodeos. He worked the bronc riding, too. Jack sometimes drove when there was a need, helped farm a little, helped with the cattle and sheep, and rode bulls at their rodeos.

Years later, Gene was inducted into the Rodeo Hall of Fame in Ellensburg, Washington.

18

The Calgary Stampede

The six performances at the 1958 Calgary Stampede took a toll on the CB broncs, but nothing lost heart and quit.

The outfit didn't take any bulls or roping stock, only one truckload of their best bares and broncs and four of Bobby's pickup horses. Reg Kesler took a truckload of broncs and a few bulls. The Canadian stock contractors furnished a truckload of broncs plus the rest of the bulls and the roping stock.

In those days the Canadians used three or four pickupmen, sometimes even five. Also, at that time the Canadian cowboys who picked up were less than skilled ropers. They could rope in the brush, but roping big teshy bulls on the fight and handling them in an arena the way Bobby could was a different story. Needless to say, he handled the bulls. With Bill Markley's help, Hank put on the Spokane rodeo and let Bobby and Bill Kunkle handle Calgary. Lucille didn't go to Calgary that year. She stayed at the ranch with Vicki.

Bobby, Jr. rode up with Bill to Calgary. Now fourteen, he was lots of help and company to Bill.

As always, Calgary was a tough rodeo and got plenty wild. Some of the toughest bronc riders around were Canadians: Winston Bruce, Less Johnson, Marty Woods, Elli Lewis among them.

Besides all the cliffhangers in the regular events there were plenty more to stun the packed grandstand in the wide-open chuck wagon races, the wild horse races, and the steer decorating.

A team of leggy bays lined up on the starting line of the chuck wagon race were climbing straight up when the gun went off. The driver's arms were spread eagle with his hands behind his head trying to hold the phobic team while the hoot loaded the camp stove. He got it loaded! The Hah horse got his legs over the Gee horse's neck and the Gee horse lunged. The other horse went down kicking. Then the Gee horse snatched the driver out of the seat and tore out! The wagon flipped, and the horse dragged it and the Hah horse, the driver, and the hoot a hundred yards before the racing team's outrider overtook the wreck and got the Gee horse shut down.

The race got off to a wild enough start to stand the crowd on their feet. Another wagon flopped over on the first turn. The team of horses behind it jumped sideways and rolled their wagon into the one ahead. There were two more wrecks before the race ended and the dust settled. It was a miracle no one was killed.

Six days of that stuff would make a man reconsider entering the chuck wagon race.

Calgary is the only professional rodeo that has a chuck wagon race. Like most rodeo events, the wild and woolly chuck wagon race stems from the daily work of the early cowboy. Although it is doubtful that the old-time chuck wagon cooks held races, it has proved to be one of the most exciting and dangerous events in any spectator sport. In the old days, the teams were made up of either plain cowpony type horses or workhorses, but in the Calgary race they are most likely high-dollar, hot-blooded, broken-down cowhands with no hankering to run a team. The drivers at Calgary are young men who live for danger.

In the past the hoot was usually a kid who drove the bed wagon and helped the cook by keeping firewood on hand and doing the dishes. Today they are usually grown men who load the cookstoves in the wagons and help the drivers.

Tuffy Federer helped Bobby, Jr. and Bill load the bucking

horses right after the bronc riding. Bobby's hind pockets were dragging out his boot tracks after the bull riding was over and they got his pickup horses loaded. Bobby, Jr. was learning the ropes of driving a semi over the road and paid strict attention after he and Bill were on the highway.

Tuffy was going to help Bobby drive home and stay at the ranch until they went to Fortuna, California, their next rodeo, in about ten days. Tuffy was all rested up and took the first shift under the wheel. He gassed up Bobby's Cadillac at Coeur'd Alene, Idaho, and drove on to Lewiston before stopping to eat.

Bobby woke up, rubbing his sleepy eyes. "Where are we?"

Tuffy cocked his hat over one eye and answered. "Lewiston. I'm gonna eat a sandwich, you hungry?" Bobby shook his head and scooted back to his sleeping position.

Tuffy ate a quick sandwich and pulled the car door open. Bobby never moved a hair. Instead of turning west on Highway 20 out of Weiser, the shortest route to the Eugene ranch, Tuffy took 95 South. They rolled into Winnemucca, Nevada, three hours before the sun awoke.

Probably the most famous cowboy hangout on the rodeo trail was in Winnemucca: Penny's. The beauties in Penny's stable outshined most Hollywood stars and New York models.

When Tuffy pulled up to Penny's and shut off the engine, Bobby raised up, looking around through sleepy eyes.

"This is a pretty good place to make a pit stop, ain't it pardner?" Tuffy asked.

Bobby was only half-awake. "Where are we?"

Tuffy slid his hat off his forehead and answered. "Hell, we're at Penny's."

Bobby brushed back his hair and put his hat on. "Who's Penny?"

Tuffy grinned. "Come on now, Bobby, don't play innocent. You've been to Penny's."

About then, the famous madam opened the door and waved at Tuffy. "Hi ya, Tuffy. Get your skinny little butt in here." She bent lower, trying to see Bobby. "Who's with you, honey?"

"Bobby Christensen," Tuffy answered.

"Well, bring that scamp in with you," Penny urged. "He's never been here, and all my girls would like to roll in the hay with one of the famous Christensen Brothers."

Tuffy turned to Bobby. "Come on, pard, there's some shinnys just waitin' to curl your toenails back."

"Where the hell are we?" Bobby asked.

"At Penny's! Come on," Tuffy answered.

"Are you talking about Penny's cathouse in Winnemucca, Nevada?"

"You got it. There ain't but one Penny's, and that's in ol Winnemucca," Tuffy answered.

"What in hell's name are we doing here?" Bobby asked, looking at his wristwatch. "The ranch is in Oregon five or six hundred miles northwest of here."

Tuffy shrugged. "Well, we're here, so we might just as well make use of my mistake."

Bobby was wide-awake now and slightly on the fight. "Your mistake? You didn't make no mistake! You didn't take 20 out of Lewiston on purpose!" Bobby said and laid his next sentence on the line quite bluntly. "If you want to fool around here, you're on your own. I'm headin' for Oregon."

Tuffy must have got hung up on some blonde's lap of luxury at Penny's; they turned his bronc out at Fortuna.

19

The First NFR

It's less than common knowledge there would be no National Finals had it not been for a Fort Worth oil tycoon named John VanCronkite.

When Bobby took part of the stock to Calgary in 1958, John VanCronkite was there promoting his idea about starting a National Finals Rodeo at the end of the season the next year.

He had already created a lot of enthusiasm throughout the West with the idea when he presented it to Bobby and Hank. He told them he wanted them to be the main stock contractors, and at Calgary he told Bobby he would have no pickupman other than him, with Lefty Wilkins and Jake Beutler. There was no problem about money or having a place to start. Dallas was perfect—and plenty of oil money was on hand.

The contractors besides the Christensen Brothers were the Beutler Brothers (Lynn and Jake), Harry Knight, Jiggs Beutler, Oral Zumwalt, Harry Rowell, Andy Jauregui, Earl Hutchinson, Bob Barnby, Tommy Stiener, Neal Gay, Cotton Rosser, Reg Kesler, and a couple of other big contractors.

Several of the men responsible for the first finals, other than VanCronkite and the stock contractors, were all Rodeo Hall of

Famers, including past World Champion All-Around Bill Linderman, president of the old RCA at that time; sixteen-time World Champion Jim Shoulders; future RCA president and Calf Roping Champion Dale Smith; the great Casey Tibbs; and Clem McSpadden, the general manager. These men had the foresight and guts to pursue the dream of making the Finals and every pro rodeo what they are today.

The immortal Jim Shoulders won the All-Around and a little cash—a mere drop in the bucket, compared to the prize money today. But along with the purse, saddle and buckle, he won an oil well, and that's not bad compensation.

The National Finals kicked up dust in Dallas for two years. Beutler Brothers had quite a few new bulls making their debut in a coliseum the first year. They were all big, longhorned bulls that fought the clowns ferociously. Most of them had to be roped and dragged out of the arena. Bobby kept a loop built, ready to rope. He was riding Rusty, the best pickup horse in his string, to drag them out. The pony was a big sorrel that could snatch an elephant across a forty-acre pasture.

In the eighth round, a big brindle Mexican cross dropped Elliott Calhoun in the well. It looked as though there was no way he could recover. The bull reversed it, picking him up, and Calhoun got a new hold. A jump or two later, the toro got Calhoun at the end of his arm, snatched the rope out of his hand, sent him out the end gate, and went looking for him.

Ronnie Rossen managed to beat the bull and got up the chutes before the bull nailed him. The bull whipped around and started clearing any human debris he could find. He freight-trained one of the clowns, then went for the other clown and flung him over the turn-back fence. He ran the judges and gate men up the chute, then wheeled, still on the hunt for victims. Bobby built to him, swinging a West Texas loop, hung it on him, and cranked on his dally *vultas,* California style. The Mexican cross had yet to learn the art of following and planted all four feet. Bobby's big horse laid on his breast-collar, turned up the steam, and, jerking the brindle behind him, headed for the stripping chute.

The rope smoked off Bobby's saddlehorn when he turned his dallies loose. The man working the gate to and from the arena didn't get it closed behind the Mexican cross. The bull boiled back in the arena and nailed Rusty, lifted his ass-end and drove him to his knees. Bobby bailed off and got up the fence. The bull plowed Rusty on, not stopping until the horse's head was wedged under the bottom bar of the steel fence. If somebody hadn't diverted the Mexican cross's attention with a hotshot and got him through the stripping chute, dragging the rope with him, more than likely he would have killed Rusty.

There was only a lift of dirt a foot deep on top of the concrete floor. A guy came out of nowhere with a hacksaw and cut the bar as Rusty got to his feet. One ear was barely hanging on and most of the hide was torn from the side of his jaw. His equilibrium was out of whack. He stood wobbling with his head hung after he managed to get up.

VanCronkite offered Bobby $5,000 for him. Bobby declined the offer. Rusty died a week after Bobby got him home.

The Finals stayed in Dallas for three years, then moved to Los Angeles.

Many of the stock contractors went on strike, in a sense of the word, and wouldn't take their stock to LA. But the Christensen Brothers, Harry Knight, the Beutler Brothers, plus ten or twelve other contractors hung in there and helped the Finals plant its roots.

The Finals flopped in LA, and the event was moved to Oklahoma City. It established colors there and found a permanent home for many years. Then, with the help of the late Benny Binion, it was moved to Las Vegas. Most likely it will never be moved again.

There's a good chance the new breed of cowboys take the Finals for granted, failing to realize what it took for the older generation to put it together and what they went through to build what it has become. The prize money, the notoriety, and the prestige of contesting there bring overwhelming crowds of people every year. It is widely known that the Finals bring in more money to Las Vegas than any other event—an estimated $10 million a day!

20

The Happy Valley Ranch

Vicki was five years old when Bobby leased the Happy Valley Ranch at Roseburg in the spring of 1962 from a finance company in LA. It was a 3,500-acre place with an older house and outbuildings. The house was a sturdy two-story affair. There was a good barn, corrals, plenty of water, and good pastureland mingling through the timber, and plenty more slowly smothering under poison oak brush. The finance outfit had traded the previous owner two or three motels for it.

Lucille brought Vicki and Bobby, Jr. to live at the Happy Valley Ranch the next spring.

There was an old cable-operated HD-14 bulldozer at the Eugene ranch, and Bobby loaded it on a flatbed trailer to pull it to the Happy Valley Ranch. Every chance he got between rodeos he climbed on it and dozed the poison oak to give the pastures a little more breathing room.

Bobby had taught Bobby, Jr. to drive anything that rolled at the Eugene ranch before he was nine years old, including the dozer.

One afternoon when the kid was pulling the friction sticks and was barely big enough to see over the pony motor, he and his dad were dragging logs. Bobby was seated on the toolbox while the dozer grunted and crawled toward a scattered conglomeration of logs ahead. As they neared one that was extra big, Bobby called to the lad over the loud engine: "You'll tear up too much country goin' around it, son . . . walk 'er over."

The dozer's tracks grabbed the thick bark on the log, lifted its nose to smell the sweet afternoon air, clawed the earth with the back cleats, and began to ease over the log.

Bobby, Jr. failed to get the clutch in fast enough to let the nose rock down gently. Instead, she flopped down with a thud under power, snorted smoke, and buried the blade.

Bobby squalled, "Throttle 'er, son!"

Bobby, Jr. jammed the throttle in, and the dozer bawled like a big bronc stud. It rooted deeper, slung Bobby off the toolbox, and shot him thirty feet through the air.

Now seventeen, Bobby, Jr. was becoming a man. There was little he didn't know about machinery, cattle, or sheep and could hold his own with the men when it came to work.

In the spring of 1965 one of the bigwigs at the finance company called Bobby after he had leased the ranch for three years and made him a proposition.

"We have decided to sell the ranch," the man said to Bobby on the phone. "We flew over it the other day and saw all your cattle and horses grazing and knew we could never be ranchers, so we're going to sell it to you."

"I don't think we're able to buy it," Bobby said, thinking it would be priced in the millions. "Not right now, anyway."

The man cleared his throat and spoke. "If I threw you a piece of steak, would you eat it?"

"It's according to how tender it was," Bobby answered.

The man pitched his price. "What does ninety thousand sound like?"

Bobby told the man he would get back to him after he talked it over with the family. Of course, everyone knew it was a steal and agreed to buy it. They decided not to borrow the bank's high-interest money for a new loan. They had remaining acreage on Green Hill where Gene Miles and Jack Halter had built their homes and thought it best to sell that land to buy the ranch. They put Green Hill on the market, but the best offer they could get was $60,000. If they waited any longer, there was a good chance they would lose the deal, so they took it. The finance company agreed to take that as a down payment and gave them thirty days to pay the balance.

When the second week in September crept up, the finance company rang Bobby's phone off the hook to make certain he and Hank knew the note was due the 26th.

It didn't take but a few of these annoying calls to quill the hair on both Bobby's and Hank's necks. Again they stayed away from a bank loan.

The Western Washington Fair was coming up in Puyallup September 17-25, a week away. Hank called the finance company to let them know he would have the money in their hands no later than the 28th, two days late. The bigwig got a little too impertinent to entertain Hank's temperament. When the committee at Puyallup wrote him a $40,000 check for furnishing the stock at their rodeo, Hank took a little plane trip to LA and practically shoved the balance, $30,000 cash, down the bigwig's throat. And as soon as it came out of escrow, they owned another ranch and combined the two on paper.

Bobby, Jr. and Bill Markley, Jr. were close to the same age, and after they graduated from high school they enrolled in college at Oregon State in Corvallis. Both majored in business. Hank's daughter, Linda, was in high school. Sherri and Vicki were still in grammar school. By the time they were in high school they were both as popular as they were pretty.

Although Bobby, Jr. had a good enough education to handle the rodeo end of the operation, he decided to ride bareback horses for a while before he got into any of the business of the rodeo company. Bill, Jr. had no inclination to ride and became a bookkeeper. His sights were not on rodeo or manual labor. He had had his fill of that on the ranch at Eugene.

The rodeos were going nonstop by this time. The Christensens had bought a new bareback horse that was very rank. He'd been throwing off every tough down the road.

One winter day, not long after they bought him, Bobby, Jr. and his dad were at the Eugene ranch, and Bobby and Hank were talking business. Bobby, Jr. had more important things than business to talk about at that time in his life and was in a bull session with the cowboys working there. They had just ridden in from moving a little bunch of mama cows from an upper pasture to the lower pasture.

"So you could ride a bareback horse?" Buck Smith said, looking at Bobby, Jr. in question.

"You damn right I can. Just take one down to the fairgrounds and I'll show you," Bobby, Jr. answered.

Chuck Shelton cocked his hat, looking at Bobby, Jr. "You think you got enough strength in your skinny little arm to hold a riggin'?"

"I can handle it," Bobby, Jr. answered.

"Wait right here cowboy!" Buck said and motioned to Sunny Johnson with his head. "Let's you and me lope to the horse pasture and gather a horse."

Gene and Bill came back with a little sorrel horse they called "What's My Line," loaded him in the horse trailer, and hauled him to the rodeo grounds in Eugene.

Bobby fit a pretty fair ride on the pony for a few jumps before he hit the ground. He knew when he got up he was going to ride bareback horses, and he turned out to be one of Oregon's finest.

Early the next morning, Bobby and Hank saddled a couple of horses to make a little circle and see if they could knock down a deer or two. They strapped a cross-buck on a pack horse and waved *adiós* to the cowboys and Bobby, Jr.

The ranch had leased the Stanley ranch, consisting of an old homestead and 2,000 acres of pasture, about forty miles south of the homeplace. Bobby, Jr. saddled up and went with the cowboys to check on some cattle there.

21

Ridin' Ol' Paint

By 1967, the Christensens' operation had grown into 60,000 acres of lease and patented grazing land and was the biggest rodeo outfit in the Northwest, possibly in the whole country.

Not counting the number of early rodeos at Crawfordsville and starting in 1936, the Christensen Brothers produced thirty-five rodeos annually:

Lewiston, ID	Puyallup, WA	San Francisco, CA
Stockton, CA	Pendleton, OR	Portland, OR
Ellensburg, WA	San Diego, CA	Toppenish, WA
Prineville, OR	Eureka, CA	Spokane, WA
Bakersfield, CA	White Salmon, WA	Klamath Falls, OR
Washougal, WA	Fortuna, CA	Livermore, CA
Molalla, OR	Roseburg, OR	Angels Camp, CA
Crawfordsville, OR	Chico, CA	Grants Pass, OR
Fresno, CA	Clovis, CA	Los Banos, CA
Red Bluff, CA	Ogden, UT	Sonora, CA
Woodland, CA	Napa, CA	Redmond, OR
Corvallis, OR	Yreka, CA	St. Paul, OR
Tacoma, WA	Eugene, OR	Salinas, CA

Monroe, OR	Bremerton, WA	La Grange, CA
Porterville, CA	Valley Springs, CA	Eagle Point, OR
Hermiston, OR	La Grange, OR	Chehalis, WA
Oakdale, CA	Woodlake, CA	Salt Lake City, UT
Redding, CA	Albany, OR	Calgary, Canada
Cottage Grove, OR	Hillsboro, OR	Sisters, OR
Caldwell, ID	Myrtle Point, OR	Salem, OR

NFR (Dallas, TX, Los Angeles, CA, Oklahoma City, OK, and Las Vegas, NV)

The Christensen ranches had some mighty good ranch horses over the years. Horses like Zeek and Charlie Brown and Miles, a pony that came out of a bucking string. Old Teddy was so rough to ride they named him after President Teddy Roosevelt, of Rough Riders fame. Sherman was a good horse, too, but if you had to lean over for some reason, he'd throw you off. And there was Lucky, Bobby, Jr.'s little horse that he and Vicki learned to ride on.

Hank was on his bulldogging horse, Charlie Brown, a big, good-looking bay, and Bobby was on Spot, one of the best cow ponies in the outfit, as they headed toward Lynx Hollow. Spot was a faithful little paint that could get around a cow fogging off a steep rocky slope with all the stops pulled.

They hit a deer trail about halfway there and followed it along behind Blackie as he sniffed for hot sign. When he hit it, he caught high gear and tore off barking out his tracks.

Bobby and Hank kicked their ponies up to a fast lope to keep Blackie in sight. The buck's tracks left the main trail after about an eighth of a mile.

Hank quit Bobby and stayed with Blackie. Bobby kept the itinerary of the main trail to circle around and get above the buck. The trail wandered along until it crossed a wide, bushy flat skirting a canyon that dropped off about seventy-five yards to a dry, rocky creek bed.

The trail cut within a foot of the canyon rim now and again. Bobby heard two shots go off. At that moment the ground broke from under Spot. He scrambled until he had nothing solid under him and tipped backward over the rim. Bobby managed to kick free when the horse turned over, his hooves slicing through the air as he somersaulted down.

A few baby trees and brush were growing from the slope of the canyon. Bobby miraculously hit one of the tender trees and clung to it. The horse hit the rocks below. Bobby clung to the tree for an hour with his fingers crossed, hoping the tree roots would hold. When Hank finally found him, he threw down his lariat rope.

When they found a place to get into the canyon a few hundred yards on up and descended in, they backtracked to the horse. It looked as though every bone in his body was broken. Bobby's saddle was torn to pieces.

Bobby was a little gimpy, but managing. When they were back on top, Hank led the way to his kill. They gutted it, slung it on the packhorse, and headed back to the Eugene ranch.

Bobby picked up at all their rodeos and at the first few finals. He was one of the greatest pickupmen ever to lift a bucking horse rider off and safely to the ground. Anyone who knows the skill it takes to pick up broncs and was around when Bobby was picking up will tell you he was among the top three ever.

To be a good pickupman isn't the only factor involved in the game. He has to be mounted well. The better the horse, the better the pickupman.

Bobby had some spectacular pickup horses: Rusty, Fifteen Hundred, Big Yeller, Little Yeller, Poker Chips, Gill, Fox, and on and on.

It was a wonder they didn't put Big Yeller in the bronc riding. He could surely turn the crank. He bucked off Casey Tibbs, Ace Berry (both World Champions), and a few more toughs when they were taking their winner's lap.

The Christensen Brothers outfit was a class act with their silver-mounted headstalls, matching breast collars, and big Garcia spade bits. Many people watch the pickupmen work during a rodeo. How they handle the stock, how they work as a team, how they're dressed—the whole shootin' match is important. The Christensens were the first to bring real color and class to rodeo.

One of the best pickup horses they ever owned was a big sorrel named Terry. They had bought him from Terry Roeser in Caldwell, Idaho. The horse had one glass eye and was a little snorty but never lazy. He had a heart the size of a number-three washtub. Terry was a Cadillac to ride and had the gas to get to a bronc, generally a bareback horse, flying down the fence like a cat with turpentine painted on his ass-end.

Without the touch of a spur, Terry would pass him at what seemed 90 MPH, stick his butt in the bronc's face, and shut him down. If a horse was throwing a fit, Terry would bail in under flying hooves for the rescue. From then on it was up to the pickupman to get the cowboy. Bob was the master at that. With an outstretched arm, palm turned back, he would sweep the rider off, around behind him and across the pickup horse's rump. All on the move, all in one graceful swipe. He carried a short nylon rope, dangling from his saddlehorn. The other pickupman would be there to trip the flank. As the bronc's head came up, Bob would slip the rope in the halter, bring the bronc around, and lead him to the catch pen.

Handling broncs in that manner not only keeps the perf moving, it saves the pickup horses and the broncs last twice as long. No other team picked up or handled broncs with that method. After Bobby introduced the style, practically every big contractor had their pickupmen doing it. No one knows why, but they all stopped doing it. Many a pickupman today has a rope in his hand while trying to pick up a rider. But the rope has no purpose, really, in a horse-riding contest. Some pickupmen have been known to drag a choking bareback horse the length of the arena to the catch pen. The only time a pickupman needs a rope is to rope a bull.

The great sport of rodeo has come a long way in recent years and yet has pushed aside so many wonderful true cowboy skills.

The collective efforts of the pickupmen and their horses play a major role in rodeo. Possibly the most important is when it comes to putting on an efficient event. A lot of time is added if the pickupmen have to chase the bucking horses around the arena for half the performance.

The crowds keep rodeos alive. No crowds, no rodeos. It's as simple as that. If hard benches and time-consuming, dust-stirring pickupmen erode the crowd to the point of exhaustion, there's a good chance it won't return for a second helping. And so the story goes.

The sponsors of the activity will shop for something that *will* hold a crowd. Neither popcorn nor sodas nor handsome cowboys—not even padded seats—will do the trick. A smooth, fast rodeo will. And pickupmen help with that.

The Christensens didn't only have great bucking horses, spectacular pickup horses, and good ranch horses, they had some uncommon, heavy-duty, athletic saddle horses anyone would want to work stock on.

The job of good horses behind the chutes plays a big part in rodeo, though most folks don't give them a second thought—possibly because they're not all prettied up and shiny like the ones in the public's eye.

Tubby was a big, soggy bay that did everything behind the chutes. In later years, when Bobby, Jr. was running the rodeo outfit, he had a big horse called Billy Bay. Like Tubby, Billy could do it all. They both worked the stock so long that if they could have read, they could have worked the stock alone! Besides working the bucking stock, they loaded trucks on these horses and dragged bales, fenceposts, wire, and whatever else needed to be moved.

As with every outfit, not every bucking horse is the rankest, and the Christensens had a couple of whips in the saddle bronc herd and two or three in their stock of bareback horses.

One bronc named Yellow Jacket threw off a pretty fair hand at Medford one year. Hank was the arena director. He rode up to the dismayed cowboy and, probably joking, said, "I can ride that twit blindfolded."

The boys at the chutes overheard the brag and bet Hank a hundred he couldn't. Naturally, he had to call the bet. After the perf was over, they ran ol' Yeller in. Hank was wearing western dress slacks, a white shirt, and a scarf tied around his neck. When he had his feet in the stirrups and his rein measured, he blindfolded himself with the scarf. Yellow Jacket wasn't rank all right, but he stuck Mr. Henry Christensen's head in the dirt in a couple of jumps, and that was the end of that story.

22

Crash and Burn

The Christensen Brothers had three rodeos in mid-September: one each in Salem and Pendleton, Oregon, and the other in Puyallup, Washington. Salem and Pendleton were at the same time and back to back with Puyallup, which began the day the two Oregon rodeos ended. Hank handled Salem, while Bobby took care of Pendleton. Hank had more stock at Salem than Bobby did. Puyallup had twenty performances and they would use all the stock there.

Hank left Salem early to get things set up at Puyallup and left the rodeo in Bill Markley's hands. When Salem ended, Bill hauled the steers and calves to Puyallup, and Manuel Enos hauled the bulls.

Bill Kunkle hauled the bulls from Pendleton to Puyallup in one load and doubled back for the steers and calves. Bobby hauled the horses and had to make a run to Salem and haul one of two loads of horses still there. He hadn't closed an eye for two days and nights by the time he got back to Puyallup with his first load from Salem.

Someone would have to bring the last load of horses from Salem. All the drivers were entered at Puyallup and up in the first perf, so Bobby had to double back to Salem. Gene, Jr., the announcer's son, volunteered to go with Bobby. He would drive back to Salem empty so that Bobby could sleep.

There was no sleeper on the truck, but it had a heater and radio, which Gene, Jr. turned on. He wasn't used to the old truck's shifting pattern and the brownie. After he came out of granny gear, he ground a couple of the remaining gears before he got it in five over. Bobby was unable to keep his eyes open. He scooted down in the seat and was asleep before they hit the highway.

It was past midnight, but Gene, Jr. was wide awake and sang along with the radio as they rattled along State Highway 99 West, a narrow, mountainous, curvy road at that time. Interstate 5 had not yet been built. There was little traffic, but the few vehicles on the road were kept backed up by the truck as it climbed the grades. The old truck was loud, and the trip ahead was going to be slow.

It was about 4:00 A.M. when Gene began to get sleepy as they rattled along the edge of the canyon guarding the Chehalis River. His eyes grew heavier as each mile passed, and he began to see elephants and all sorts of weird things as he fought to keep them open. No matter how hard he tried, he couldn't do it, and his chin hit his chest.

The truck swerved and headed for the edge of the canyon. The trailer brakes were rigged to come on if the tractor and trailer ever disconnected, and when the tractor left the highway, the trailer brakes howled and smoked. The trailer skidded to a stop before it went over. There happened to be a police car a mile or so behind the truck, and the policeman saw it go over.

Bobby woke up as the tractor sailed though the air. It nose-dived into a pile of huge boulders about fifty feet down. Both doors popped open, and Gene, Jr. flew out, crashing against the rocks. The truck bounced off its nose, burst into flames, and flipped. The radiator, fenders, and engine curled under the cab. Bobby had gone through the floorboard and was crunched up next to the engine. The flaming truck turned over and over in midair until it landed on a giant boulder in the river. The splash of water blew the fire out.

The truck hung up on the boulder and settled. Bobby was penned, but was able to keep his head above water.

The policeman who had seen the wreck was stopped where it went over and was out of his car, looking into the canyon.

When Gene, Jr. came to, he saw he was only scratched up and he climbed to the top. The cop couldn't see him in the dark. When Gene, Jr. appeared out of nowhere, he nearly spooked the cop out of his wits.

"Where in the hell did you come from?" the cop asked.

"I was drivin' that truck," Gene answered.

"Was there anyone else in the truck?"

Gene lit a cigarette and answered, "Yeah, there was another guy in it."

"Well, we don't have to worry about him. He's dead for sure," the cop said and radioed for a wrecker in McKenna, a little town about four miles south.

The wrecker driver took a little dirt road in the canyon that ran along the riverbank. The driver stopped his truck when he reached the site of the wrecked truck. He positioned the wrecker where he could hook on to Bobby's truck and pull it out. Then he waded up to his waist to get his hook and cable out to the wreck.

When he saw Bobby, he yelled. "Are you dead?"

"Nope. I'm okay . . . Can you get me out of here? I'm penned in!" Bobby answered.

The driver hooked on to the wreck, waded back to his wrecker, and dragged his torch back. After he cut Bobby out, he couldn't believe he had survived the crash.

23

The Blizzard of '69

The eight December nights outside the coliseum during the 1968 National Finals Rodeo in Oklahoma City packed a wallop of freezing cold.

The rough stock riders didn't experience much of the weather, except maybe a slight nip walking to and from their cars to the rodeo or from their rooms to the bar. But the timed-event contestants got a pretty good dose of it, brushing, saddling, feeding, and watering their horses and waiting for their runs in the long, cold alleyway leading into the building. The men working the stock and the labor list in the pens outside didn't have it nice and cozy either, but they got the job done with no whining.

Ronnie "Punch" Rossen was one of only three men to ride all eight head of bulls. He made a supernatural ride in the last go, on a big red bull. Three jumps into it the bull jerked Rossen down and spattered his face with the blunt end of a tipped horn. Blood burst from Rossen's head.

The bull came around to the right and into Rossen's hand. Rossen threw his weight out of the well and went on. The bull wrapped it up until the whistle blew. Rossen got his wrap, bailed out, and went to his knees. The bull snuffed at him and found the open stripping chute gate.

The stretcher crew loaded Punch into the ambulance. It took 300 stitches for the emergency room doctor to patch up his face. But Rossen had won the round, and according to him it was worth it.

Hank and Bobby had already experienced many a slippery winter trip across the Texas Panhandle on old Route 66. To be concerned for the truck drivers and stock was natural. They were older and wiser than Bobby, Jr. He was a little reckless in those days, along with the two new drivers.

After Bobby, Jr. and the trucks rolled through the metropolis of Amarillo, as well as Wildorado, Vega, Adrien and Glenrio, all tiny Texas cow towns, and crossed into the Land of Enchantment, Bobby and Hank were able to breathe a little easier. Still, they knew the long haul across New Mexico and Arizona wouldn't be a piece of cake until they reached Kingman. And it wasn't.

They breezed through the village of San Jon, on through Tucumcari, Montoya, Cuervo, Santa Rosa, and then Albuquerque, Grants, and Gallup. There were a few windy flurries of snow along the way, but nothing big until they hit the sixty-mile stretch between Winslow and Flagstaff, Arizona. Twenty-five or so miles before they reached Wynona, trucks and cars were stretched out for miles on the sheet of ice glistening over 66.

Several vehicles were stranded in the deep banks that had been bladed off by snowplows. Motors were running so loudly you could hear nothing over the roar. Cars were turned sideways; trucks were jack-knifed. Men bundled in heavy jackets battled tire chains with nimble fingers to put them on. The Christensen truck drivers were accustomed to the chore of chaining up.

The red lights on police cars and the yellow beacons on wreckers looked like a string of Christmas lights stung along the highway. It took eight hours before the mess was cleared.

When the rodeo outfit got home from the NFR, it was cold—

but nothing compared to what it had been from Oklahoma City to Kingman, Arizona.

When January rolled around, the weather turned nice, at least on the West Coast. But on January 29, it hit: the biggest blizzard anyone living in Oregon at that time had ever seen. Forty-two inches fell at the Eugene ranch and thirty-eight or so at the Happy Valley Ranch.

Nothing mechanical on either ranch could move. All the regular vehicles were buried—the flatbed, the pickups, the Cadillacs, and Mollie's new Buick. The big trucks were locked in the snow up to the windows of their cabs. The exposed batteries on the tractor and old dozer had frozen and busted. There was nothing anyone could do but sit back and wait for the sun to come out, but it didn't. It continued to snow for a week.

The Christensen ranches had pasture leased all over the country for 3,000 head of sheep. Five hundred head of ewes and lambs here, and five hundred head there. The livestock were stranded in bunches everywhere.

Bill Fletcher, a bronc rider who worked for the outfit occasionally, packed hay to the stock on packhorses, slinging two bales on each. The snow was so deep and blinding, the only way he could tell where the stock was stranded was where the snow had melted from the heat of their bodies.

There was so much livestock stranded that Bill Fletcher couldn't get to them all. Bobby, Bobby, Jr., Hank, and Bill Markley started packing hay on the ranch horses, the pickup horses, and the flag horses.

On the Stanley ranch lease, near Midway and Oakland, two little burgs between Roseburg and Eugene, there were 500 head of ewes that had been on tall green grass and had a healthy crop of lambs on the ground when the storm hit.

Bobby telephoned the Hutchinson Equipment Company and rented a D-9 Cat with an operator to come clear the roads into both the Happy Valley and the Eugene ranches, then go to the Stanley place to bulldoze a road into the sheep. The operator dozed the road in as he went.

When he arrived in the pasture where the sheep were, the first thing he did was fall off in a swale. He had no way of knowing it was there under the thick blanket of snow. Bob called for another dozer. All that operator could see when he reached the stuck Cat was the smoke chugging from the smokestack; the rest of the dozer was buried in the snow. The operator was sitting in the pickup with Bob on the road he had plowed in.

Both operators fought with stiff cables and stiff fingers and tore a big hole in the snow and mud in a futile attempt to get the stuck dozer out for two hours. Finally, the tracks of both dozers grabbed enough solid ground to get the stuck Cat out.

After the snow melted a little on top, Bobby rented a D-8 and then plowed a few roads for people who had been stranded in their homes for ten or twelve days with no way to get out for firewood or groceries.

The bucking stock, steers, roping calves, and saddle horses were safe in the pastures nearby where they could be fed easily. But the ranch animals had to be fed by helicopter.

Sixty head of cattle froze to death on the north Umpqua lease. Also, every buck sheep at Happy Valley and everything on the lease land near the outskirts of Winston had frozen.

Unable to get enough hay packed in, they hired a helicopter for $100 an hour to drop hay to the stranded stock still alive.

Before it was all over, they had lost 1,200 ewes, an untotaled number of lambs, sixty cows, and eight barns. Jim Lewis lost 1,200 head of sheep in his sale yard.

The catastrophe lasted for thirty days. When spring finally came, the ewes that had survived the blizzard began to lamb. Their lambs were dying right and left. The milk in the ewes' bags had frozen in the storm. But the inherited traits passed down from two young Bohemian ancestors gave the Christensens the foresight and ambition to rebuild their empire. And they did.

Bobby, Jr. married Kathy Tomley and old Clint Hall died that year of 1969. He had become part of the family, having lived there in the house for over thirty years. He and Mollie grew old together after Pops died. They buried him with a military funeral at a little pioneer cemetery on the south end of the home ranch. Of course, the soldiers played taps, and the cattle, up and down the canyon, started bawling. They kept it up until taps was over. It was chilling.

As in all families, there are days of sorrow and days of ecstasy. The Christensens had known many of both.

24

The Higgley Hop

A few days before the rodeo in Clovis, California, during April in the middle 1970s, they turned out all the broncs in the field to let them exercise. At this time Bobby, Jr. was Hank and Bobby's main man at putting on the rodeos. When they came to feed the following morning, about three-quarters of the bronc herd was gone. The gate had opened mysteriously. The search commenced—but no horses.

Late that afternoon the police arrived with good news. They had seen a remuda in a rundown old grape vineyard about a half mile down the freeway. Bobby, Jr. saddled reliable old Billy Bay. Another cowboy saddled up. They loped down the edge of the freeway and there in the vineyard, as big as you please, were the escapees grazing away. Up popped their heads at the sound of two riders coming, and they knew they'd been caught. The two cowboys got around them and squalled. But the broncs didn't need to be pointed; they knew exactly how to get back to the rodeo grounds and did so in a medium to fast lope.

The rodeo outfit had plenty of insurance to appease the squawking old man who owned the vineyard, and that was handled.

The grapes must have added a little iron in the broncs' blood.

They flattened about half of the riders in every perf. The bulls pancaked ninety-five percent of the ox crotchers. That called for a celebration, and old Clovis came alive that night when the boys had their insides oiled up good.

They had a week before Porterville. It would start on April 30, so they had plenty of time to sober up. Porterville was one of their very first California rodeos.

The Christensen Brothers had become a household name in the world of rodeo, and the family was well acquainted with scores of movie stars—big stars who longed to escape the lunacy of Hollywood.

Many stars had found refuge at the Eugene ranch in the thirties and forties to spend a week or weekend in the green paradise of fresh, clean mountain air and taste the dust on a real working ranch. Will Rogers, Hopalong Cassidy, Hoot Gibson, Gene Autry, Slim Pickens, John Wayne, Gary Cooper, Audie Murphy, Edgar Buchanan, and James Stewart were a few of many.

Later, Steve Ford, the son of President Gerald Ford, rode bulls and rodeoed with Bobby, Jr., and Bobby, Jr. helped the president campaign against President Carter.

Cecil Andrus, the future governor of Idaho for thirty years, went to college at the University of Oregon, and every summer he helped Mollie hay at the Eugene ranch until he graduated.

Senator Wayne Morris visited Mollie many times, as did Mack Baldridge, President Reagan's secretary of commerce, who was later killed in a roping accident at Jack Roddy's ranch in California.

Throughout the years both the Eugene and Happy Valley ranches had served as a second home to many a wandering cowboy. All were well-known names in the rodeo world. They would just stop and spend a few days filling up on home-cooked meals.

The ranch was no dude outfit where only hired hands work. It was a cow and sheep outfit, and the visiting cowboys who hung around worked. They weren't told or paid to; they worked because they were built that way.

To mention just a few in the early days: Stub Johnson, Mac

Griffith, Bob Cook, Sonny Tureman, Eddie Akridge, Jess Ferguson, Leonard Macravy, Bill Linderman, Pete Crump, Paul Templeton, Larry Daniels, Steve Johnson, Chuck Sheppard, Yakima Canutt, Tom Bride, Stub Barnham, Cotton Rosser, Buddy Peak, Sammy Flinn, Buck Smith, Tuffy Federer, Vern Cathcart, Rolfe Graham, Mel Lambert, Jackie Wright, Ross Dollarhide, Johnny Mitchell, Johnny Hawkins, Duane Howard, Jim Roeser, Manuel Enos, Ralph Lamb (the sheriff of Las Vegas for over thirty years), Benny Binion (owner of the Horseshoe Hotel and Casino in Vegas), Bill Ward, Ike Thompson, Jack Bushbolm, and Casey Tibbs. Casey always showed up ready to work in his purple satin shirts, satin scarves, and starched Lee jeans.

As the years progressed, new faces and names in rodeo began to show up: Benny Reynolds, Bob Edson, Ronnie Rossen, Ronnie Raymond, Bert France, Mart Woods, Walt Mason, Russell McCall, Ken and Bill Stanton, Ace Berry, Jack Roddy, Lee Markholt, Larry Kane, Doug "Droopy" Brown, Larry "Bull" Mahan, Louie Zabala, Clyde Vamvoras, Andy Miliate, Randy Corley, Bobby Delvecio, Danny Tatum, Stan Harder, Buzz Sealy, Jim Custer, Bobby "Hooter" Brown, John and Jim Ivory, "Cody Bill" Smith, Jim Houston, Frank "Machine Gun" Kelly, Monty "Hawk Eye" Henson, Jerry Hixon, Chuck Shelton, Carl Schnabele, Vergil Neves, Shorty Horn, Wayne Hill, Bill Kornel, Bob A. Robertson, Mike Isley, and scads more. Way too many to mention.

Somewhere along the way, Bobby, Jr. invited fifteen or twenty cowboys to the Happy Valley Ranch after the Roseburg rodeo. Bobby Delvecio and Randy Corley were there, as were Albert Vandorn, Buzz Sealy, Hawk Eye Henson, Hooter Brown, Bull Mahan, Droopy Brown, and the rest of the gang. (The nickname Droopy doesn't exactly fit Doug Brown's style. He was college educated at Corvallis with Bobby, Jr., and, as well as being one of the classiest World Champion bronc riders in his day, he had more taste in dressing than most of his breed.)

Bobby, Jr.'s wife, Kathy, served food and made sure there was plenty of Bud and Coors handy, some Cokes, a little Cutty Sark, and a splash or two of "CB" brandy for the coffee. A local band provided the music.

Like most get-togethers, the party broke out of the gate slowly, but after the "Knock 'em Down John" took hold, it didn't take long for the night to get wild.

Somebody killed a Coors and suggested they go down to the corral and get on some of the wild cayuses. After the troop staggered to the pen, Bobby, Jr. roped three or four of the gentlest broncos out and stacked his wood on a saddle horse. The others led the broncs up on the gravel road, where the party was under way in front of the house. Bobby, Jr. snubbed them to his horse.

New York City transplant Bobby Delvecio got on the first one. A few years later, and a few thousand more miles on down the road, he was wearing the Reserve World Champion Bull Riding Buckle. His bull riding skills failed to help much on the bronc: he only lasted a jump or two. The booze may have had something to do with his flight.

Somebody else chugalugged a beer and climbed aboard another bronc. He, too, kissed the stars somewhere out in the "Wild Blue Yonder."

An Arizona team roper, Howard Nichols, was on hand, but not primed quite well enough to stick his Tony Lama curb kickers in a set of oxbows. Nichols hailed from a humongous cotton patch in Higgley, Arizona. Thus derived the title the Higgley Hop.

The music was getting louder and the night shorter when some bird down the canyon phoned. Hooter Brown answered. The guy told Hooter if things didn't quieten down he was going to introduce the whole bunch to his double-barreled scattergun.

"Well, get your butt up here and we'll see just how tough you are," the Texas flash retorted coolly. Hooter was nobody to fool with; he meant what he said. Not only could he fisticuff, he could shoot straight when he wasn't on tilt. Just to be on the safe side, in case the guy on the phone was some sort of crazy, Hooter got his .44 from his van.

The clock was ticking. The gunfight was drawing closer. Tension was building as "High Noon" neared. As the sky in the east was beginning to lighten, the music grew mellow and cowboys were snoring. Hooter was practicing his draw. "Watch this, boys," he said to a couple of cowboys still standing but leaning against the front yard fence.

Hooter drew his gun, clicked back the hammer of the .44 in the motion, and a blaze of fire shot from the barrel. The bullet ripped through his Wranglers and blew a hole in his leg. They rushed him to the hospital to find that it was only a flesh wound. Hooter and Hawk Eye were able to make it to Hollywood to be guests on *The Tonight Show* with Johnny Carson. They would have to burn a little rubber and cross a few double lines along the way to get there in time, but they would make it.

Meanwhile, back at the ranch, the boys were waking up. "Well, looky there," Bobby, Jr. said, pointing out the broncs grazing lazily along in the noonday sun, all still dressed in bronc saddles and all dragging platted reins through the tall grass.

"Well, wouldn't that make you buck your bridle off?" Buzz Sealy said as he attempted to smooth down his rat nest of blonde hair.

What a night they had! And it was that very night that the Higgley Hop became a tradition on the ranch.

25

St. Paul and Molalla

Along with Bobby and Hank, Bobby, Jr. was as busy as a junkyard dog putting on St. Paul and Molalla over the Fourth of July. The two Willamette Valley farming towns, around twenty miles apart, made it an easy run.

The job of running the two rodeos on the same date was nothing new to the Christensens; Bobby and Hank had handled St. Paul for twenty-five years and Molalla twenty-nine. Bobby, Jr. had ridden in and out of the two arenas since he was belt buckle high to his dad.

Fans flocked to St. Paul from Salem and Portland, both within a thirty-minute drive of the rural community.

The Molalla rodeo was secondary to St. Paul. The arena at Molalla in those days was in bad shape, nor was the seating the best.

Bobby was picking up with Stub Bartelmay at Molalla in the early fifties. A bareback horse threw someone off, and the two pickupmen were racing beside the bronc. Bobby was on the inside, ready to run his little rope through the halter. Stub was against the fence, crowding in to trip the flank. They were in line with the roping box. The bareback horse bumped Stub's horse, knocking him into the front of the roping chute. The horse went down and straight over, landing on Stub, then scrabbling to his feet, shaken. Stub was curled up on the ground, motionless. A herd of cowboys chased behind Hank as he spurred his horse toward Stub. Bobby laced his rope in the loose bareback horse's halter on the run, tripped the flank, turned him into the stripping chute, and spurred to the crowd ganged around Stub. He stepped off his horse like a calf roper as the pony slid to a stop.

A doctor dashed out of the grandstand. Stub had swallowed his tongue and torn his shoulder out. The doctor pulled his tongue free, but the shoulder was so far out the doctor couldn't get it back in. An ambulance pulled up, and two attendants put Stub in and took him to the hospital. He only lived about another month.

Stub was the best pickupman Bobby ever worked with. They were a highly skilled team and coordinated down to a hair. There have been few pickup teams in all of rodeo that could compare with them.

In 1935 a few St. Paul farmers and businessmen envisioned an annual Fourth of July rodeo in the circular City Park. The park, active with hustling summer league baseball players on a diamond surrounded by scotch broom, was large enough to add a quarter-mile horse track, four bucking chutes, and a roping chute.

On July 2, 1936, St. Paul kicked off the first perf of the ever-enduring rodeo with a long, colorful parade down the main street and a fine grand entry in the new arena.

William "Bill" Smith furnished the broncs for the first three rodeos. He passed away late in 1938. Harley Tucker of Joseph, Oregon, got the contract and furnished the stock for the St. Paul Committee until his passing. After he died, Hank Christensen bought Harley Tucker's stock at a dispersal sale for close to $40,000. That move led directly to the Christensen Brothers being awarded the St. Paul contract.

The rodeo grew in leaps and bounds between '39 and '55. The committeemen hiked the purse up considerably, installed lights for night performances in 1940, and built a new covered grandstand. They added six bucking chutes and a set of bleachers for more seating in 1945. The grandstand was increased to a 7,000 seating capacity in 1955, and the bleachers were increased to accommodate 3,000.

When the 1962 Columbus Day storm blew in off the Pacific Coast at about ninety knots, it drenched the town, rattled the chutes and grandstand, and played hell with the bleachers. They built new bleachers the next year and new chutes in '64.

The run between St. Paul and Molalla was a snap for the cowboys. There were always a bunch working them both. Along with the pros, there would always be a gang of weekend cowboys. The big leaguers also made the summer rodeo at Klamath Falls, but few of the weekend hands added Klamath Falls to their run. Klamath Falls was practically the length of the state from the other two.

As the years trotted along, the St. Paul and Molalla toughened up, but the twisters got tougher. Klamath Falls was right along with them. Every cowboy who ever took the sport to heart worked all three at one time or another.

Bobby and Bobby, Jr. were waiting when the big Christensen Brothers trucks rolled into St. Paul the morning of June 30, 1962. Every driver who ever herded a Christensen Brothers truck down the road was a cowboy and knew the ins and outs of handling stock. Bobby, Jr. had the holding pen gates set before the trucks arrived. Bill Markley was on hand for the trucks at Molalla. Bobby, mounted on Billy Bay, was waiting down the alleyway that split the pens when Bill Kunkle arrived in the first truck with forty head of bareback horses.

Backing a fifty-five-foot trailer to line up the narrow tailgate with a three-foot-wide unloading chute ain't cotton candy, but Bill Kunkle had it down pat, he had done it for so many years. Bobby was inside the chute when the trailer gently bumped it and stopped. Bobby, Jr. raised the tailgate on the trailer. The

Kenworth grumbled and belched when Bill shut off the engine and climbed out of the cab.

The first bronc smelled the floor of the chute before he stepped out of the trailer, and the others followed. Bobby turned them into one of the holding pens and shut the gate on Billy Bay. Every saddle horse in the outfit was broke to open and shut gates on.

After the saddle broncs and bulls were unloaded and penned, Bobby treated the crew to breakfast at the Swept Wing. Hank had rooms reserved at the motel there and had breakfast with them.

Bobby, Jr. and his dad picked up. As usual, Hank was the arena director. Salem's favorite son, Mel Lambert, announced.

Ace Berry led off the bareback riding on One Spot to set the pace with a score in the high 70s, but Jim Dix won the average. Stan Schricker had hell in the calf roping and Dean Oliver won it. Larry Jordan got by Jeremiah in good shape, but J.C. Bonine won the bronc riding. Ray Lovell won the wild cow milking. Probably the best bullfighter ever, Wick Peth, took Corkscrew off of Chris Johnston at St. Paul that year and saved a bunch more. Snuffy had a good day with Jim Charles, but Jim didn't have a good day with him. A little bench-legged, *choppo*-built Indian bull riding specialist, Larry Condon, won the bull riding.

Marilyn Camarillo was the barrel racing champ, and Dan Torricellas, a Eugene cowboy, won the steer wrestling and the Presidents Trophy for the All-Around.

Bobby, Jr. was worn to a frazzle after he returned to the Happy Valley Ranch. But he perked up when his and Kathy's second daughter, Rebecca (Becky), was born on July 7. They already had Michelle when little Becky was born.

Life on the ranch was running smoothly, with never a dull moment; a new adventure was always at hand.

One morning when Michelle and Becky were in grade school, Bobby, Jr. saddled up to help some other cowboy gather the bull in one of the pastures at the Eugene ranch. It was nearing noon and Bobby, Jr. was making a circle in a lope when he saw a pretty good-sized dead log blocking his path. His horse leaped, and on the other side of the log was a baby fawn. She jumped up under his horse and he nearly went down. Bobby, Jr. held him up by the bit and turned in his saddle. The fawn was wobbling, straddle-legged, with her big brown, curious eyes wide open and her little rapid tail waving.

Bobby, Jr. lifted his bridle reins to shut his horse down and stepped off. He had to take mousy little steps to get up to the baby and be real gentle about picking her up and carrying her to his horse. It was sort of a chore to lift her on his gelding. The horse rolled his eyes around, snorted a time, and sidestepped a time or two, but Bobby, Jr. managed to get the fawn laid across his saddle and mount.

He had a soft spot for animals, especially little wild ones. He and Vicki were always trying to catch them. They did lots of times and made pets out of them. They had a coon named Lisa, a fox called Matilda, and an assortment of other creatures running around the yard.

Bobby took the fawn home to the Happy Valley Ranch and gave it to Kathy and the girls, who named her Bambi, of course, and nursed it with a bottle. When she was three or four months old, they halter broke her then talked Bobby into letting them take her to rodeos with them where they'd tie her to the trailer to get used to strangers.

After she got to be a yearling and was big enough to make it on her own, she would just hang around the house like a dog. The girls would let her come in the house now and then. On one such occasion she strolled into Bobby, Jr. and Kathy's bedroom and lay down on the bed. When they tried to get her off the bed, she stood and peed, but wouldn't budge. Her hooves were sharp and she was dangerous to get rough with. It wasn't long afterward that Bobby earmarked her and turned her loose with a few wild does.

One afternoon when Bobby, Jr. was taking Kathy and the girls to town and driving across the pasture, there was Bambi and another doe. They could tell it was Bambi by the earmark cut in her ear. Bobby, Jr. stopped and Becky and Michelle jumped out of the car and started yelling at Bambi. About that time, some guy pulled up behind the car in a pickup and stopped. The two does started bouncing toward the car. About halfway there, the other doe stopped, but Bambi kept coming. When she reached the fence, she gracefully sailed over it and jumped right into the back seat of the car.

Becky and Michelle were hysterical and jumped in with her.

When Bobby, Jr. finally pulled the doe out of the car, the guy in the pickup started shaking his head in disbelief and told Bobby, Jr. he'd never seen anything like that, and if he told anyone they wouldn't believe him.

26

Other Great Christensen Brothers Broncs

War Paint was born on the Klamath Indian reservation. His sire was a big, raw-boned, hammer-headed paint the Indians could never break. His mother was a cranky old mare they drove in a team. They never tried to break her to ride, and she was too poor and old for the Christensen Brothers to try out for a bucking horse.

Orrie Sommers owned the old mare's last colt, War Paint, a leggy, agile, paint yearling.

When the Christensen Brothers saw the yearling's potential, they bought him from Sommers. He bucked for thirty years and was the bucking horse of the year three times. Decent, a big yellow bronc in the Beutler Brothers herd, won it five times.

The following is a quote from the August 1, 1966, edition of the *Rodeo Sports News*.

> War Paint, the first horse to be awarded the silver mounted halter indicative of the title Bucking Horse of the Year. He won the honor three times. He was retired by his owners, Hank and Bobby Christensen, July 10, at the Emerald Empire

Roundup in their hometown of Eugene, Oregon. To a standing ovation the big paint bucked off his last adversary, Jim Bothum, and was unsaddled in the arena . . .

Seen by more people than the great racehorse Man O'War, War Paint has had fan mail from all over the world. Henry Christensen estimates War Paint has traveled some 540,000 miles across the United States and Canada . . .

One of the toughest bronc riders in the sixties, Bill Matinelli, had this to say about War Paint: "Other guys talk about how tough the big horse was to ride. He throwed me off fourteen times."

After the great horse's death at thirty-two, he was taken to a taxidermist, then inducted into the Pendleton Rodeo Hall of Fame.

Miss Klamath was inducted into the PRCA Hall of Fame in August 1998. Why War Paint was never inducted into the PRCA Hall of Fame in Colorado Springs is a puzzle to many bronc riders. He was one of the greatest saddle broncs to ever crack his hocks over his head. They didn't initiate the bucking horse of the year award and silver mounted halter until 1955. War Paint was the first to win it. He went on to win it in 1956 and split it with a Harry Knight bronc named Jake in 1957. In those days no other saddle bronc had won it that many times.

One winter afternoon in the middle sixties, Chuck Shelton, a bronc rider and rodeo secretary for the Christensen Brothers for years, was at the arena in Eugene along with some other cowboys. A guy brought in a little spoiled bay horse and asked if they would like to try him.

Sonny Tureman got on him with a saddle and found that the little horse was double rank. Shelton hustled over to Hank's daughter, Linda, who was there watching. He had her write out a check for $300.

When Hank saw him buck he didn't hesitate to give Shelton back his $300. They named him Smitty—quite appropriately since the man who sold him was named Smith. Smitty might not have been one of the most famous bucking horses that ever lived, but he was one of the best that ever came down the pike. He went to the National Finals sixteen times and went both ways, as a saddle bronc, thirteen times, and in the bareback riding three times.

In 1975 the top fifteen saddle bronc riders had a halter made for Smitty. It was silver, inlaid in gold, and engraved "To Smitty, small in size but big in heart. The uncrowned Bucking Horse of the year."

In the spring of 1974, Shorty Horn, a northern Nevada cowboy, brought a load of killers to Caldwell, Idaho, for Hank and Bobby, Jr. to look at. Manuel Enos and Bobby, Jr. tried them out.

When they ran a little *choppo*-built horse in the chute, Bobby, Jr. got on him with a bareback rigging, and he bucked pretty good. From their point of view, Hank and Bobby saw potential in him. They had Manuel try him with a saddle, and he was an exceptional saddle bronc. The others were only average. They bought him and called him CheckMate. His heart was bigger than his body, and he went on to win the saddle bronc of the year that very year.

It was a few years later that they began to crown the outstanding bucking stock in the other events with the honor. Prior to that time only saddle broncs were awarded.

A guy named Able in McDermott, Nevada, called Bobby and said he had a horse nobody could ride. Often when somebody has a horse nobody can ride, only local cowboys try the horse and are thrown off, and they think he's double rank. Such was the case here, and Bobby didn't think the long drive would be worth it.

The guy called Bobby constantly to come look at his bronc until he wore Bobby out and he decided to go and look at the magnificent animal Able was bragging about. He took Jerry Hixon with him. Jerry was a saddle bronc rider, and a pretty salty one at that.

When they got to McDermott they met Able at a thrown-together arena, which had only a couple of chutes. The leggy, thin, high-withered Palomino was standing in one of the chutes.

Jerry had to set his saddle three inches behind the break of the horse's neck to keep it from going over his head. He took a wild horse rein and slid down in his saddle, confident that he could handle "old Yeller." He was wrong. The bronc threw him off. When he came walking up to Able and Bobby, dusting himself off, Able said, "Wadda you boys think now?"

"I'd like to try him again," Jerry said.

"You can try him as many times as you want, but you won't ride him!" Able said, accenting a tone that struck a determined note in Jerry. He cinched his tree on five more times and watched his stirrups flopping over his seat five more times, as he sat on the ground watching that yellow son-of-a-buck kick on down the arena. He got on the yellow horses six times that day, and six times the horse had rung him out.

Bobby bought the horse and named him Mr. Smith after Gene Smith of the St. Paul rodeo committee. They bucked Mr. Smith in the bronc riding six or eight times. He was pretty light-headed, and when a bronc rider would pull on his head he'd go to spinning. He couldn't throw anybody off when he'd spin, not unless he threw the saddle off, too, so they put him in the bareback riding. He was so thin and long-withered that if you didn't set your rigging way back on him, it would go over his head. He'd buck like hell for a few jumps with a bareback rigging, and if it started up on his neck he'd fall into a spin. Even if you were able to sneak by him you couldn't win anything on him. None of the bareback riders wanted him in the draw. Bobby, Jr. was pretty much running the outfit and turned him out for a year.

After the year was up and Mr. Smith had put on a couple of hundred pounds, Bobby, Jr. told his stock foreman, Bill Stanton, that he was going to take Mr. Smith to Oakdale. Bill threw a wild horse fit. He hated the yellow son-of-a-buck and let Bobby, Jr. know it in no uncertain terms.

Lo and behold if the current World Champion bareback rider, Jack Ward, didn't draw him in the slack at Oakdale. There was no doubt in anyone's mind that Jack Ward would flog Mr. Smith, but they all knew he wouldn't win a dime on the sorry son-of-a-buck.

Jack sat on him, watching, until Bobby, Jr. picked up the bareback rider in the arena. When he had the horse out, Jack heated his rosined glove on the handhold, worked his hand in it, scooted up, and nodded.

Ward could flat spur one and come a'spurring for about five jumps, but it was *adiós*, Mr. Ward, when Mr. Smith bucked off the champion. He rode right-handed and bucked off on the left side, landing on his feet with his hand hung in the rigging. Extremely athletic and as agile as a cat, Ward grabbed a handful of mane, sprung back up on the bucking horse, got his hand out of the rigging, and jumped off the other side.

Well, that started it for the sensational Mr. Smith, whom they renamed Smith and Velvet.

The following year he went to the finals and was voted the third best bareback horse. Within the next six years, he was named the bareback horse of the year four years in a row.

Not too bad for a rangy old nag.

27

The Right Doctor Might Have Saved Her

A million diamond-studded stars, hanging out with the big Oregon moon, were sprinkling magic over the sweet spring night. Bobby's arm was strong but gentle around Lucille as they danced over the shiny hardwood floor at the annual fireman's ball. They had danced across the same floor thirty-eight years earlier. *It doesn't seem possible,* she thought. She didn't feel any older, although she knew she looked it. Except for the pain that had been nagging her for the past couple of weeks, she was as spry as a young filly.

When the dance ended, Bobby was ready for the next one and held her hand to keep her on the floor. "You sure haven't lost your touch, honey," he said. "Are you ready to go again?"

Lucille smiled faintly. Her eyes told him she would rather sit down. "Your back's hurting, isn't it? Maybe we better go to home and get you to bed."

"It's not that bad," she said. "We can stay a little longer. I would rather sit this one out, though."

Bobby spoke as they walked back to their seats. "Are you sure you don't want to go home? It's okay with me; I have to leave for Salinas early anyway."

Lucille smiled. "Let's wait until the band takes a break."

Her pain kept her awake most of the night. It was worse that night than it had been since it had started.

Bobby blamed himself for urging her to go to the dance in the first place. And about all Bobby could do each time she woke was gently pat her back to sleep.

Bobby, Jr. had already taken the stock to Salinas. Vicki went with him. Like her father, she had no idea her mother's pain was more than a normal backache and that having her husband or daughter close might comfort her. Lucille wasn't one to complain.

The rodeo at Salinas would start July 14, two days later, and end on the 17th.

It was long past midnight when Bobby got home and found Lucille in dire pain.

The following morning he took her to a doctor in Roseburg. The diagnosis was disturbing. He discovered a tumor and told Bobby it was possibly cancer.

"If it is, what then? Can you do anything?" Bobby asked.

The doctor told him they couldn't be certain it was cancer without operating. "If it is, it may not be malignant," he continued.

"What did Lucille say?" Bobby asked.

"I didn't tell her. I felt it was better that she didn't know. I did tell her I would like to do an exploratory operation."

Mollie came to the hospital with Bobby the day they operated.

The doctor's affirmation was blunt when he found them in the waiting room. "It's malignant." He continued by saying there was nothing that could be done, and that she only had, at best, just weeks to live.

Bobby wouldn't settle for that and set out to find another doctor.

Francisco Zamora, a performer out of Mexico who trick roped at many of the Christensen rodeos, was married to Mildred Zamora. She was formerly from Texas and had a clinic in Tijuana, Mexico. She had discovered a treatment for cancer, but the United

States barred her from practicing. She helped many Americans who had come to her clinic in the early stages of cancer.

In desperation, Bobby rushed Lucille to Tijuana. Mildred told Bobby that if they had not operated, the cancer would not have spread as rapidly and there was a good chance Lucille would have lived as long as ten years. As it turned out, the clinic was only able to prolong her life for a year. She died in November 1974. Bobby had lost his best friend and the only woman he had ever loved.

28

Hawk Eye, Bull, Droopy and Hooter

The last day of the Umpqua Valley roundup at Roseburg in 1976, Hank received word that he had been inducted into the Cowboy Hall of Fame in Oklahoma City.

After the rodeo they had their annual Higgley Hop, and the aura of companionship hanging over the Happy Valley Ranch was stronger than ever. The party had grown immensely. Previously there were always a hundred or so people there, invited or not. That particular year there were over four times that, mostly cowboys as usual—the whole Columbia River Circuit among them.

After the barbecue and some dancing, Bobby, Jr. joined Ricky and the Red Streaks on stage, where the famous band was getting down with their Little Rock and bluesy music. Bobby, Jr. borrowed the microphone to announce the news of Hank being inducted in the Hall of Fame. Hank got out of his chair, hot footed to the stage, and took command of the mike, saying, "I'm dang sure not going for it if they don't put Bobby in, too." It was short and sweet, but he meant every word.

This was not a kinship where one would grab the glory and leave the other out. There was a deep affection and camaraderie between them, a profound love and ever-enduring commitment to each other. Bobby, Mollie, and the rest of the family had to do some tall talking to get Hank to change his mind and accept the honor.

Bronc riding remained a tradition of the annual Higgley Hop. Well into the night Bobby, Jr. rounded up the boys and headed for the corral. While he gathered ten head of second string broncs out of the pasture on a saddle horse and drove them in the corral, the boys were constructing a circular, headlight-lit arena with their cars fifty or so yards from the party.

Back at the corral they helped Bobby, Jr. put bronc halters on the broncs and led them to their shiny fender and hood arena. Bobby, Jr. snubbed the first one. Somebody crawled on him. Three, maybe even four jumps, and the cowboy took wing.

Doug Brown cinched his tree on the next one and roweled him from the mane line to the cantle.

Hooter mounted up, hat whipped and spurred until his bronc kicked a headlight out of somebody's new Buick.

Bobby, Jr. snubbed a big hook-nosed bay for Hawk Eye Hensen. After the second jump the bronc decided he'd go to the party and bucked over the hood of a car. Panic struck in the party when they heard the bronc's hooves clip the car hood and looked up to see him headed straight for them.

Hank knocked over his chair scrambling to his feet and ran out throwing up his hands to redirect the bronc. The bronc almost flattened him and bucked on. He scattered people, dogs, tables, chairs, sleeping bags, paper plates and cups, a stack of oak firewood, the cook, barbecue rib bones, potato salad, cornbread, pinto beans, three tubs of beer and Cokes, two full garbage cans, and remnants of liquor bottles everywhere.

Hawk Eye's trademark feather stayed planted in his hat as he whipped and spurred the bronc, squalling every jump: "Buck and bawl, you wild son-of-a-buck!"

29

The Lovely Trick-Riding Christensen Girls

Two years before, in the spring of 1972, when Bobby's daughter Vicki graduated from Douglas High, she flew to San Mateo, California, for an interview at Hughes Airwest. Being that she was only seventeen, they told her she had to wait until her next birthday before they could hire her.

As most young people do when they turn eighteen, Vicki decided to route her goals in another direction and abandoned her pursuit of an airline career to find a new goal. That usually is not an easy decision to make; it's one that a smart girl takes her time in making. So she decided to work at the ranch and rodeos while she thought about it.

Hank had three beautiful daughters. Peggy, the oldest, never rodeoed. Linda, the second to the oldest, barrel raced and trick rode. Like her older sister, Linda, the youngest daughter, Sherri, had inherited a love for rodeo from her father and also became a trick rider. She, Linda, and their cousin Vicki grew up around their father's rodeo outfit, washing pickups, washing, brushing and saddling pickup horses and flag horses, cleaning and bedding stalls, soaping and oiling saddles, running errands, feeding the dogs and stock, taking care of the tack trailer, and carrying flags in the grand entry.

If the outfit was short-handed, they would work the gates for the men sorting the broncs and bulls.

Vicki was crowned Miss Rodeo Oregon and went on to win the horsemanship award in the Miss Rodeo America contest in Las Vegas. When it came to riding a horse, Vicki could make anyone stand up and take notice.

Following the Wayne Newton show at the Frontier Hotel and Casino, a well-known comedian named Jackie Kahane, acting as master of ceremonies, crowned Miss Rodeo Nevada—Pamela Martin from Las Vegas—as Miss Rodeo America of 1973. Today Pamela Martin is the well-known television commentator known as Pam Minick.

At the 1974 Salinas rodeo, one of California's biggest, a trick rider was unable to ride. Vicki volunteered to take the injured rider's place. She had never attempted the challenge but was confident she could handle it.

There would be only four straight runs in each perf for each trick rider. The other riders included Sherri Christensen, Connie Griffith and her young son Tad, Jimmy Medearis, Liz Lorimer, Bonny Happy, Edith Happy's daughter, and Lex and Torri Connelly's daughter, Danielle. Torri was married to Ken Curtis, who played Marshal Dillon's sidekick "Festus" on *Gunsmoke*.

Vicki had had secret aspirations to trick ride for years. Her dreams got to the point that she bought a well-used trick riding saddle. In her spare time on the ranch she would saddle a gentle horse, slip through the timber to a wide meadow, and practice a few self-taught tricks.

After making the commitment to stand-in at Salinas, she cinched the old saddle on Sonny, one of Bobby's well broke pickup horses, and executed her chosen stunts without a problem.

Sherri and Linda had been blessed with the same attributes in beauty and skill as Vicki. In addition to those elements they were both seasoned trick riders and had preformed nationwide.

By this time, Linda had married Lee Markholt, a tough Oregon bull rider, quit trick riding, and turned her secretarial genius to the rodeo outfit. She and Lee had two daughters, Anna and Amy.

After Salinas, Sherri and Vicki decided to put together a trick riding act and go on the road. Vicki had everything it would take to be a professional. She was an above average athlete with an intrinsic knack for showmanship.

Before Sherri had begun trick riding, she met Lyndi Irwin, from Nuevo, California. Lyndi had been trick riding with Dick and Connie Griffith for quite some time. Dick and Connie were two of the best in the business. Linda Christensen had ridden with Dick and Connie in the early to mid-1960s, and they taught Sherri to trick ride also. Sherri was selected to travel to Old Mexico and perform with the troupe of Tony Aguilar.

While practicing for the tour, she pulled all the ligaments in one knee to the ankle. In another incident she sustained an injury while practicing a stunt at the ranch. Her horse was flying down the fence and hit the brakes. Sherri kept going and slammed into the barn, breaking more than the boards.

The idea of trick riding in rodeo was a concept that came into existence from the circus. Every other contest in rodeo originated in the arena except for the saddle bronc riding and roping. The bull riding is a catch colt from steer riding, a practice no cowman would have allowed on the cattle drives where rodeo itself was born. When a bull calf is cut he becomes a steer and loses his fight—or masculinity, if you prefer.

Cowboy contests on the open ranges of yesteryear came to town and were dubbed with the Spanish name *rodeo*, pronounced ro-*day*-o. But town folks soon grew tired of the monotonous repetition of bronco riding and roping. Rodeo promoters, hungry for gate money, asked the men providing stock to add more events—and thus steer riding came into being. The old longhorn steers weighed up to 1,500 pounds and bucked with just enough zest to gratify the public.

After rodeo had grown into a major audience draw in the pre-1920s, the big Texas longhorns had vanished from the scene. They were replaced by little weak steers, hardly big enough to buck a kid off. In order to remedy the dilemma, many contractors tied firecrackers to the steers' tails, a dismal failure in an effort to make them buck harder. Bull riding was the only alternative.

Most fans think that bull riding is the roughest event, but they are wrong. Bareback riding is by far the roughest; bull riding is the most dangerous.

Bareback riding derived from the early Indians breaking their horses to ride with no more than a mane hold and a leather string in a horse's mouth. Streams, rivers, and lakes, with the water up to a horse's belly, are hard places for a horse to turn on the power, so the Indians broke them to ride in water. Aware of that fact, a light came on in someone's head at an early rodeo, and bareback riding became a contest.

Performing tricks (trick riding stunts) hasn't always been a specialty act. At the time of its birth, just after the turn of the twentieth century, it was a competitive event, as was trick roping. It was judged on the hazards of the stunts and the costumes worn.

Most anyone who's ever been to a rodeo knows that the phenomenal black cowboy of Austin, Bill Pickett, invented bulldogging (steer wrestling) by throwing 1,200-pound steers with his teeth.

Many of the stunts of that era were extremely dangerous and are rarely done in modern rodeos. The event was removed from the ranks of competition sometime in the twenties and became a specialty act.

While Linda, Vicki, and Sherri were busy growing up in the rodeo company, they hung out on a lot of arena fences watching their fathers and other cowboys compete. Witnessing the agility of accomplished trick riders such as Dick Griffith, J. W. Stoker, and astonishing, incredibly pretty female trick riders like Nancy

Sheppard, Connie Griffith, Edith Happy, Donna Hall, Karen Vold, Corine Williams, and Rosa Lorimer set the stage for Vicki and Sherri. The fascination of the colorful, graceful dexterity in trick riding aroused the passion in the young girls to perform.

After the Salinas run, Sherri and Vicki decided to go on the road. When they began to put the idea in motion they felt a three-girl troop would be superior to a two-girl act. They contacted Lyndi Irwin and presented their idea to her. She moved to the ranch, and the trio was formed.

After months of practice, under Lyndi and Sherri's supervision, Vicki was ready. They worked up a format and went into rehearsal.

When the Rodeo Cowboys Association convention came up, concurrent with the rodeo in Denver, the fabulous Christensen trio Cadillaced to the frozen city and filled their dance card with committees to perform at as many big rodeos as they could—rodeos other than the ones using Christensen Brothers stock. Those were in the bag, but the girls could only take the ones relevant to their schedule.

They worked rodeos at Ellensburg, Washington; the Fort Worth Fat Stock Show and Rodeo; Cody, Wyoming; Lewiston, Idaho; the Pacific International at Portland's Expo Center; the Rouge River Roundup in Medford, Oregon; the Redding Rodeo in Redding, California; the rodeo at Oakdale, California; the Oregon State Fair at Salem, and more.

Vicki met Danny Tatum, an aggressive young cowboy from the cattle country in Arizona. His father, Dick Tatum, was looking through a cow-horse's ears before he could walk. One of Danny's sisters, Dixie, married Jim Custer, a tough bareback rider until he was sidelined with an injury. Danny and Vicki were married in 1976 and moved to the ranch to work when they weren't rodeoing.

In 1978 Vicki became pregnant. She decided to quit trick riding and devote her time to her family.

Brett Tatum was born in the fall of that year, on September

22, exactly one month to the day before Bobby, Jr. and Kathy's only son, Jesse Cole, was born.

Sherri gave up trick riding in the early eighties and married Rob Smets. They had two daughters, Josie Dee and Sammie Jo.

Part Three
On Top of the World

30

On Down the Road

From their humble beginning during the depression, the Christensen family scratched and clawed their way to become one of Oregon's most powerful commodities in the sheep and cattle industry by the early 1980s. And they put together one of the biggest rodeo outfits that has ever existed. Fifty years of backbreaking work!

Both the Eugene and the Happy Valley ranches were wealthy in patented and lease land all over southern Oregon.

The rodeo end of the operation climbed to the prestigious position of being the largest stock contractors in the Northwest and was neck and neck with Harry Knight, Harry Vold, Tommy Steiner, and the Beutler Brothers for putting on the fastest and most colorful rodeos in the world. If anyone else, at that time, had the notion they could handle a rodeo better than these three giants could, they had better come with both barrels blazing.

Cowboys in every era of time between the late twenties and eighties worked the Christensen Brothers rodeos—from Earl Thode, recognized in 1929 as the first World Champion All-Around Cowboy by the RAA (the first organized rodeo union or association, if you prefer) to the two unrivaled All-Around

Cowboys, Larry Mahan and Tom Ferguson. Both broke every All-Around record set in the hundred-year correlation to rodeo with six titles each.

All of these men deserve recognition as the great athletes they were. The devotion and skills of good riders continues today. A recent example is an Arizona kid named Ty Murray, who had been riding since he was in diapers. Literally. His dad, Butch, held the seat of his pinned-on britches as he ran alongside bucking calves to hold the little squirt on. Ty was kicked in the head when he was two, ending up with a concussion, but neither that nor anything else could stop him from jumping out to win seven PRCA All-Around titles when he was barely old enough to shave. It's a shame this magnificent young athlete wasn't around to challenge the tremendous bulls and bucking horses in the Christensen Brothers string.

Those tremendous bulls included Snuffy, NFR ten times; Wilfred, eight times (and bucking bull of the year in 1966); Missoula, seven times (bucking bull of the year 1967); Oscar's Velvet, five (bucking bull of the year 1983); and Trouble Shooter, NFR six times. Other CB bulls that went to the NFR between one and five times were Snowman, Sleepy, Droopy, High Noon, Big Ed, Geronimo, Iceman, Tommy, White Hope, Nitro, Rapid-fire, Whirlaway, Playmate, and Wolf Guard.

And there were Mt. Man, Big Red, Ground Split, Floyd Cook, Sox, Velvet Playmate, Flintstone, and Pale Face. They had a bull they named Life after a picture of him was put on the cover of *Life* magazine.

Ike Sanky rode Oscar's Velvet at the finals. He was the first man to ever make the whistle on him. Oscar's Velvet was the calf of the great Oscar and a Black Angus cow. Oscar was featured in the Academy Award-winning documentary *The Great American Cowboy*. Oscar came out of the Bob Barnby string when he sold out to Bob Cook, Jack Roddy, and Jack Sparrowk, Rodeo Stock Contractors (RSC). The Growney Brothers, John and Don Kish, bought RSC out in 1979, but Bob Cook kept Oscar. Bobby, Jr. gave Cook $15,000 for Oscar's Velvet.

Almost every contractor today has a pen full of bulls in the same category. But in case any of you bull riders out there ever wondered about a CB toro, I'll tell you. You had to have your hammer cocked and your riding pants on when you took your wrap on one of their bulls. There were plenty back then who did: Harry Tompkins, Jim Shoulders, Duane Howard, Billy Hand, Ronnie Rossen, Joe Green, Kenny and Bill Stanton, George Paul, Bill Kornel, Phil Lyne, Donny Gay, Bobby Steiner, Denny Flynn, Randy Magers, Butch Kirby, Bobby Berger, Sandy Kirby, Ike Sanky, Lane Frost, Jim Sharp, and Jerome Robinson were only a few.

Christensen Brothers NFR bareback horses were Three Corners, Mighty Mouse, Smokey and Strawberry Shake, Woodburn, Burt River, Brown Tee, Smitty, High Society, War Dance, Teacher's Pet, Red Devil, Simple Simon, Quick Change, Party Doll, Mr. Smith, Big Al, Billy Buck, Bimbo, Legs, Country Cousin, Jack of Diamonds, Little John, Misfit, WineGlass, Capone, Tee Pee, ZX, Golden Glow, Sassy Sue, Bo Jingles, Dandy Dan, Red Lady, Rusty, Checkmate, Fancy Velvet, #11, Sitting Bull, Spider, National Velvet, and John Wayne.

There's no doubt today's bronc riders have ridden and bucked off as many great saddle broncs as the ninety-three head of CB NFR broncs, but none have ever been on anything ranker than War Paint, three times bucking horse of the year.

Not to discard the overwhelming ability of any bronc rider, dead or alive, who may have chanced to punch it out on Miss Klamath for ten seconds, starting with Juan Lavvis and Harry Brennan to Dan Mortensen and Scott Johnson, the qualifying time was ten seconds when this old mare pitched. As I mentioned earlier, she was only ridden one time in five years.

Juan Lavvis was the first All-Around Cowboy and Bronco Buster at Prescott, Arizona, in 1864. Harry Brennan was crowned the World Champion Bronco Buster at Cheyenne in 1904.

The above statement covers a lot of territory both in time and men. As the saying goes, "There was never a man that couldn't be throwed nor a horse that couldn't be rode." But Miss Klamath had yet to be born when that saying came about.

In the time of the RAA, formed in 1928, all the stock contractors who were affiliated with the association furnished saddles, and these saddles were called "association saddles." The stock contractors pretty much controlled the association, so you rode with their saddles. Most of the saddles were plain old using saddles with great big swells that practically wrapped around a man's legs, or "traps." Some even had steel horns. It made no difference if a contractor handed a cowboy a fourteen-inch seat and the guy needed a sixteen. Tough! You rode what they gave you.

A few stories passed along by old-time bronc riders are unbelievable. According to Turk Greenough, if you were a tough bronc rider, in the estimation of some stock contractors, they wouldn't let you ride with chaps. Joe Orr said if they thought a rider was tough enough to ride a certain bronc, the contractors would smear axle grease on the swells of the saddles. The cowboys had no say-so. The late Turk Greenough and Joe Orr are both great uncles to the 1993 World Champion Bareback Rider, Deb Greenough.

The CTA (Cowboys Turtle Association), the Turtles, came into existence in 1936. A few years later the cowboys went on strike at Boston. No cowboys + a full house = no rodeo. The strike, commonly called "The Boston Garden Petition," organized rodeo and laid the foundation of what rodeo has become. The cowboys won! Along with the hike in prize money, including adding entry fees to the purse, they wrote other new rules that expanded into the RCA, which in turn spawned the PRCA.

There is bad and good in everything, and not all contractors were crooks.

Like all stock contractors in those days, the Christensen Brothers furnished the saddles, made by Hamley, the top saddle maker in the world. (Every once in a while an old Hamley will turn up at today's rodeos.) Every bronc rider that worked a Christensen Brothers rodeo knew that there wasn't any bull going on with them. If their broncs couldn't throw a man off fair and square, it was ridden anyway.

There was a little bronc rider in the sixties named Larry Kane. Only he can tell you why he rode with a concoction of "Heat" and "Castor Oil" when he cracked out in the pros. He would glom it on his chaps and swells, making it all but impossible to get him on the ground. Everyone started using the goop—at least, everyone who thought they needed a gimmick. It slipped by until the RCA wrote a rule that would result in disqualification if a rider were caught using the concoction.

Larry Kane rode just as well without it. When he discovered he didn't need a gimmick, he ended the year as the rookie bronc rider and went on to become one of the best in his time.

Long, long time ago they used plain cotton ropes instead of bareback riggings. The first riggings were nothing but a piece of leather with a strap anchored on them. California bareback rider Pete Dixson made the first really good rigging. The body and handhold were thick double skirting leather, and he may have been the first to put rawhide in the handhold. World Champion Jim Houston modified the old Dixson and set the stage for other cowboys, such as World Champ Bruce Ford, and various saddle makers to build different versions until the perfect rigging turned up.

World Champion Johnny Hawkins made the first pair of *good* bareback riding spurs. They are the granddaddy of the bareback riding spurs of today.

31

The Hot Red Fire Engine

Cowboys cornered the knack of "whoopin' 'er up" way back when the West was really wild in places like Wichita and Abilene, Miles City and Great Falls, Deadwood and Fargo, Deer Trail and Denver, and Prescott and Tombstone.

When the shipping pens came in sight, the worn out ol' longhorns were too tired to pull off a stampede at the sound of popping six-shooters, squalling cowboys, and the cordial declaration of train whistles, announcing the news that the beef had arrived.

The new breed of cowboys are a little more passive than their forerunners and have tamed down their celebration of victories considerably. Throwing their hats, waving their arms, and hugging their pals is a little more civilized—but not near as wild and fun.

During the Christensen Brothers reign in arenas throughout the Northwest, the cowboys still knew how to whoop and stomp, and occasionally things got a little *too* western.

One year at the Cowboy Reunion in Milton Freewarter, the present hometown of Butch Knowles, a few of the boys cut loose in a bar and went to fighting with the locals. Among the cowboys were some damn tough northern boys: Jackie Wright, Ronnie and Rick Raymond, Buck Smith and his brother, Cicle Swaggert, Tom

Murray, Mac Griffith, and a couple more. After the battle had a pretty good start, here came the law. The first puncher they captured was Ronnie Raymond. After they cuffed him to a telephone pole, he went to kicking, spitting and cussing, and the cops went to billy clubbing.

One of the cops jerked out his pistol and leveled down on Jackie Wright. Buck Smith's brother slipped around behind the cop and tied him up in a bear hug. Jackie got a dead lay at the cop and punched him out. The cop shot into the ceiling. When they finally got the war stopped, they locked Buck Smith and Tom Murray in the bar and threw the rest of the toughs in jail. And there they sat. Sick, sober, sorry, and plenty bruised up. After they stewed for a couple of hours, Larry Kane, the little Montana bronc rider whom all the boys thought was a flash in the pan, bailed them out.

The next day, Sammy Flynn, another rammin' jammin' bareback rider, came driving up to the rodeo in a little red convertible and parked right up next to the fence. The rodeo went along without any complaints until the bull riding. About halfway through it, a bull bucked somebody off, headed straight for the fence, jumped it, and landed square in the middle of Sammy Flynn's shiny new convertible. The top was up and intact when the bull landed, but it was torn to pieces as the bull stood there half in the back seat and half in the front, daring anyone to challenge him.

After the first perf at Portland, one of the Christensen Brothers' major rodeos, a few cowboys got tanked up and decided to steal a fire engine. There was an old relic on display in a vacant lot near the fire station. It looked as though it had been parked there since the state was a territory. The cowboys snuck up in the night and climbed on the antique. Clyde Vamvoras got behind the wheel, and someone found the crank and began twisting. It probably hadn't been started since 1910. The old mama finally sputtered, popped, belched a cloud of smoke a few times, and actually started. Wild grass and weeds had grown up around the skinny rotting tires, but they had enough air in them to keep the spoke rims off the ground.

One of the cowboys found some dusty old fire hats and passed them out. The boys raked out the cobwebs and buckled them on. Vamvoras turned on the red light, someone grabbed the bell rope, someone else found the siren, and it was "Show Time!" Vamvoras gave her all the spark and gas she had, and the old gal lunged, chugging out of the lot, and down the street they went.

With red lights flashing, the bell ringing, and the siren whistling they clamored all the way to Vancouver, Washington. When they got her parked, the bellman gave the bell a few more jerks in front of the bar at the motel where they were staying and they went in, fireman hats and all. The bartender bought them a drink. The patrons bought a few more after they went outside and crowded around the old gal to look her over.

Three or four cops arrived the next day on the hunt. A band of thieves was reported to have been spotted speeding through the streets of Portland in an antique fire engine. After the police parked their cars up next to the arena, they came marching into the arena—ready to draw just in case the criminals made a run for it. The grand entry was about to begin. The cops started looking for the thieves in the long line of riders. Mum was the word, and the cops didn't get to arrest or shoot one single felon.

32

The Pendleton Roundup

Trailing behind the turn of the century, when the great cattle drives were only memories of the Wild West, and the old-time punchers had left it in the hands of history, rodeo was nothing more than a few buggies, some little putt-putt cars and a handful of mounted riders forming a big circle around the bucking horse and roping contests.

The summer of 1908 had been nothing but long callusing days in the leather for the cowboys on the high Oregon plains, and it was time to go to town and oil up on "who shot John."

The cow ponies were dinked and the boys were dragging out their boot tracks with their hind pockets, so the ranchers around Pendleton put their heads together and decided to have a rodeo so the cowboys could whoop off some steam

"We'll call 'er the Pendleton Roundup," one of the ranchers said, and so began one of the top-notch rodeos in America.

The bucking horses were furnished by the ranchers. With no chutes, they had to snub the broncs, which got a little wild. But that didn't make much difference to the cowboys—they got a little wild and woolly, too.

Cowboys were a breed apart, and not the smite of the broncs, nor the rules of town, nor the process of the law, nor the sting of the whiskey bothered them.

Those old broncs were a far cry from the broncs of today. They would stand on their hind legs and slap the snubbing horse's ears flat, paw the hat, hair, and eyebrows of the man on him or try to bite his arm off. Mostly wild horses, they were straight off the plains where the high desert wind blows. They had drunk the bitter water, run with the deer, fought fangs of winter and claws of the cougar, and had followed the eagle to the high rocky nest.

There were no such things as flanks at that time. If a pony couldn't throw a man off, he was just liable to rare over backwards and drive the horn of the bronc saddle though a man's heart.

No arena was built in Pendleton until 1910. The grandstand was full when the sounds of the big booming band joined the waves of heat in the air, and a long parade of cowboys and cowgirls rode into the arena. The riders wound around the American and Oregon flags as the announcer shouted into his megaphone introducing the who's who in the Grand Entry. Ben Jory, Guy Weadick, and Thad Sowder were there to compete against Sheridan, Wyoming's pride and joy, Harry Brennan, along with the famous Nez Perce bucking horse rider, Jackson Sundown, and several other top bronc stompers.

Hoot Gibson, the silent movie star, won the All-Around Cowboy honors.

Without hobbling her stirrups, Bertha Kapernik made an exhibition bronc ride. The following year, the first year women were allowed to compete at Pendleton, she won the women's bucking horse riding. In 1912 she won it again and returned in 1914 to take the title once more.

Many a track has been made in that old arena and many a spur rowel has turned; many a *caballo* has been forked and many a kid mesmerized.

Bobby and Hank got the contract to furnish the stock at the Roundup in the late fifties and had it for over thirty years.

Some great cowboys and some *damn good* ones have been added to the Pendleton Roundup Hall of Fame. One of the greatest was an Oregon boy named Larry Mahan, inducted in 1998, ten years after Bobby Christensen was inducted.

Henry (Hank) and Bobby, Sr. were inducted into the PRCA Hall of Champions in 1989, along with Casey Tibbs. Hank had been inducted into the Cowboy Hall of Fame in Oklahoma City in 1984, and Henry was named the Rodeo Man of the Year in 1982.

The three-performance rodeo in Ellensburg, Washington, started in 1923. The Christensen Brothers got the contract there in 1950 and had it until 1988.

Henry and Bobby were inducted into the Ellensburg Rodeo Hall of Fame in 1999 and the St. Paul, Oregon, Hall of Fame in 2000. War Paint was inducted into the Ellensburg Rodeo Hall of Fame in 2001.

33

The Cow Palace

Starting in the early fifties, the Christensen Brothers' great bucking horses and bulls performed at the Grand National Livestock Exposition and Rodeo under the lights in the Cow Palace coliseum at California's biggest rodeo for many years.

The roaring crowds watched War Paint, Miss Klamath and her filly colt, Miss Red Bluff, buck down many a great bronc rider at the Cow Palace. Casey Tibbs, the best in his time, was one. They were all tough bronc riders, the best in their day. Miss Klamath was never ridden over four jumps at the Cow Palace.

Oscar's Velvet and Wilfred, two outstanding Christensen bulls, always trotted out the catch pen gate under the applause of the excited crowds: both had flung all the champions off at one time or another.

There were some outstanding rides and buck-offs on old Rattly Bang, Smith and Velvet, and Smitty in the bareback riding at the Cow Palace. Rattly Bang, a big, arm-jerking gelding, wasn't around long but he was double rank. One year a tough bareback rider from Arizona named Arnold Jones had Rattly Bang at the Cow Palace, and the big horse jerked Jones' arm out of the socket.

The Cow Palace was the last major rodeo of the year, and the list of contestants topped the mark there every year. Hank and Bobby always had to hire subcontractors to have enough stock to go around. They used well-established rodeo outfits like Andy Jauregui, Cotton Rosser, Beutler Brothers, and the Big Bend Rodeo Company.

Cotton had some good bareback horses there. One he called Short Fuse was a snappy, short-legged, mutton-withered sorrel. He'd just jump and kick and didn't have a duck in him, but he was very stout and it took a "Popeye" arm to ride him. (The author had him twice and he got the riggin' both times—but he didn't have his nephew Deb Greenough's "Popeye" arm, he said.)

Short Fuse was rank enough to throw off guys, but bareback horses like Smith and Velvet of the Christensen string could certainly bring the big boys down.

Every pro contractor has good horses, but it's doubtful anyone has ever had as many as the Christensen Brothers. Sling Shot and High Tide of the Flying U String were two more good bareback horses. Sling Shot was a big, stout bay gelding that came around to the right cracking 'em. You'd better have your hammer cocked or he'd get you.

A big thoroughbred of Lynn and Jake Beutler called Snappy John had only been qualified on four times in the eleven years he bucked. He was hell to get out on, and Sonny Linger, their chute boss, had to hang a right-handed gate on if it was a left-hand delivery or he'd go over the gate.

Twelve Bells, Little Dan, and Waffles were three of the best to draw out of the Beutler Brothers herd, but they had a bad cat they called Gooch, a big, black half Percheron-looking horse with his ears cropped. If you could make the whistle on him in pretty good shape, you could place. If he threw you off or the pickupmen dropped you, and you didn't beat him to the fence, he'd lay his stub ears back and run you down, snapping his teeth like a timber wolf.

Andy Jauregui had a good-looking sorrel thoroughbred called Red River. A rider could get way up in the nineties on him if able to spur him out and make the tooter. (The author won Ventura, California, on him with a 191.)

Andy had three other great bareback horses to get a check on at that time. WhizBang was a little buckskin you could win first on if he didn't brad you to the back of the chute. Empty Saddles was a 1,300-pound palomino that jumped and kicked as straight as a string. And there was ol' Cheyenne. Most guys would have killed to draw him. He was a big brown and white paint and the kind that every bareback rider dreamed of having. His back was a good foot and a half to two feet wide and he didn't have much for withers, but he bucked with his head up and your rigging stayed put if you had it pulled right.

You could ride him with one finger. Literally. Once, Elliot Calhoon bet Andy a hundred that he could ride him with one finger at Parker, Arizona, and he did. It was like sitting on a cloud; he practically spurred himself if you were tapped, but if you were a little ahead or behind him he could buck you off.

When Cheyenne died, there had been more money won on him than any bucking horse in history.

Empty Saddles and Cheyenne were nice bareback horses to ride, and also like every contractor, Hank and Bobby had some nice ones to ride, but most of them were a far cry from pups.

In 1972, Bobby, Jr. was having his best year in the bareback riding and drew Flying Us Slingshot for his first one at the Cow Palace. He hadn't been ridden yet that year, but Bobby, Jr. conquered him for a big 66 points, but at least he hung to him. He had Cheyenne in the second round and took the victory lap on the big paint. In the third round he had Diamond Spur from the Big Bend Rodeo Company's pen and made the short round. He had Headlight in the short round. Headlight was a big, raw-boned sorrel out of the J spear outfit's pen, Andy Jauregui's herd, and a piece of cake he was not. He came around to the left and hung Bobby, Jr. on the top rail of the coliseum wall. So much for winning the Cow Palace!

A couple of years later, Bobby drew a big yellow CB bareback horse they called Chicken Hawk. Bobby knew him well. He wasn't the most desired horse to draw, but he could buck pretty fair. It was getting out on him that was sticky; he'd mash a guy if he wasn't tied in real solid. By this time he'd broken every leather halter they laced the ropes through to tie him in. That wasn't the best remedy, so they started tailing him. That kept him on all fours until they jerked all the hair out of his tail. He placed the fear of God in every bareback rider. And it certainly wasn't a crime for them to turn him out, but Bobby couldn't very well turn one of his own horses out. T.J. Walter can tell you all about how bad Chicken Hawk was in the chute.

They kept moving him up the night Bobby had him. His turn was quickly approaching and the sweat was running over his sideburns. There were only two left to go when Jim "Blades" Ivory appeared on the scene with a great big rope.

"He'll mind his manners when I get his head cinched to the gate with this rope," Jim said and anchored Chicken Hawk to the gate. "The only way he'll turn over is to pull the chute out of the concrete."

Bobby, Jr. winked at Ivory and spoke. "That rope's big enough to hold an elephant down with two wraps and a hooy."

When the arena was clear, Bobby slipped down on Chicken Hawk and nodded. Jim turned the rope loose when the gate swung, but the elephant rope hung in the halter when the horse bailed out.

The Christensen kid was concentrating on the spur-out rule and didn't see the dragging rope with a knot tied in the end of it. He had his rowels planted over the breaks, and things were looking good. One jump completed. Then one and a half and the loose end of the knot in the rope hung in the gate, and Chicken Hawk did an "allemande right" and the rope came loose from the halter. Bobby, Jr. made the corner, but Chicken Hawk won the round. Bobby, Jr. did a double reverse flip and landed right in front of the chutes with his feet straight in the air.

A rider could win first on any bronc the Christensens had— or any of them could throw you off. (The author had their big, blazed-faced sorrel, High Society, at Ogden one year and slopped a ride on him for third. If he hadn't hung and rattled for eight, they would have only paid first and second. Only three made the whistle in the round.)

Hank was the arena director, and during the calf roping he tied ol' Mickey up behind the chutes and went for a cup of coffee. When he got back, his saddle was turned around backward. Henry laughed about it with the cowboys who had pulled the prank.

It was election year for the PRCA and anybody with good sense would have been on their best behavior. But not any of these guys—they were an ornery bunch, to say the least.

Before the last perf somebody brought a big poster of a stark-necked, long-haired hippie and hung it right out in front where the whole audience could see it. On it was a sign that read "Nasty Bo Ashhorn for President." Bo was a bull rider who could take a joke with the best of them, but the board of directors didn't think it was all that funny.

The Cow Palace was a fun rodeo. One year, still in the 1970s, a bunch of them went to the "Cowboy Bar and Café," got drunk in the bar, and started a big pie-throwing contest. John Edwards, a long-legged NFR bareback rider, and a couple of more got suspended over the deal.

Plenty of Wild West hands were around in those days, but there never was a better bunch of guys. Whoopin' and hollerin' was a big part of rodeoing back then, but the new gladiators on the rodeo trail nowadays get down to business. I'm glad to see that the new breed is showing the pubic that cowboys can handle whatever is necessary. And tending to business is necessary in today's world.

One year in the early 1970s, Bobby, Jr. received a call from Bob Thain, a partner with Dave Johnson in Thain-Johnson Enterprises, an entertainment promotion outfit in Santa Cruz, California. The company put on concerts and circuses and other big events around the country. Thain told Bobby, Jr. that they were interested in putting on a rodeo in Santa Rosa, California. It sounded like it might work, so Bobby, Jr. took a trip to Santa Cruz and located Thain-Johnson Enterprises. Bob Thain was a big man, dressed professionally. He invited Bobby, Jr. to take a seat and they began to discuss the matter at hand.

It just so happened that the Cow Palace would be going on the same dates as they had planned for Santa Rosa.

After he agreed to take the contract, they agreed to pay Bobby a month before the rodeo.

Albert Vandoren and Bill Stanton were working for the Christensen outfit. Bobby, Jr. sent Albert to run the rodeo at Santa Rosa and took Bill to the Cow Palace with him.

When Albert got to Santa Rosa, he called Bobby, Jr. in San Francisco and told him there was not one thing advertising the rodeo. Not a sign, nor a poster, nothing. It didn't even look like there was going to be a rodeo that weekend. Bobby, Jr. told Albert not to let it worry him; he already had the check in the bank. He told Albert to go ahead and take the stock to the arena, put them on feed and water, check the bucking chutes, and see if he could locate one of the judges to help him set up the barrier at the roping chutes. If nobody came to the rodeo, it was their loss. If only one fan showed up, at least the cowboys would have an audience.

Albert found a judge and had everything ready to go when the cowboys started dribbling in. And before long, the bleachers were full.

Bob Thain and Dave Johnson had advertised over the radio and sold tickets over the phone. They sold so many that they had to add a performance.

Bobby, Jr. and Bob Thain went on for years putting on rodeos together, and Bob would have every seat sold out six months in advance.

Later on, Bob Thain started booking rodeos in Hawaii every year on Thanksgiving. Cotton Rosser helped put on the rodeos. There was already rodeo stock there, which kept Cotton and Bobby, Jr. from having to ship their stock over. Cecil Jones was always there to help out with the rodeos. Casey Tibbs was there some, and being a celebrity didn't stop him from helping with the work. There were some good Hawaiian cowboys there, and still are. Mostly timed-event men. One in particular was Stanley Joseph, the All-Around of the little Hawaiian Rodeo Association.

It was a nice vacation for the two contractors and their wives. Everyone always had a good time. Along with the rodeo, they did some sightseeing, a little beachcombing, enjoyed the nightlife, and had rickshaw races. Casey Tibbs, Bob Cook, and Jerome Robinson put together a couple of rodeo tours and took their troops to Japan. As anyone who has ever rodeoed knows, the humdrum monotony on the road gets old. So getting to fly off somewhere to have some fun and rodeo too is good for the soul.

In 1980 the Black Velvet Whiskey Company became one of the main sponsors for the PRCA. They put on two rodeo tournaments, one in Las Vegas and another at the Nassau Coliseum in Long Island, New York.

Bobby, Jr. took his stock to New York. Jim Sutton of Sutton Rodeos, Inc. and Bob Cook (representing RSC and Cotton Rosser) were two of the other contractors. Cook was also the manager of the affair. Bobby, Jr. and Steve Sutton picked up broncs.

Bobby Delvecchio, the only NFR bull rider ever from the Bronx of New York, was the big star. The attendance was good and gave the New York folks something to watch besides Broadway shows.

Following the last perf on a Sunday afternoon, Black Velvet put on a big awards party to present $10,000 for the best bucking animals of the year. Delvecchio borrowed a saddle horse and took him up to the cocktail lounge on the third floor in the service elevator to let the fans pet a real western-type horse while he signed autographs.

34

The Diamond Horseshoe

John VanCronkite had given Bobby a diamond horseshoe ring to show his appreciation for the job he had done at the first NFR at Dallas. Since that time, Bobby never took it off or had it appraised.

One afternoon, when he was sixty-three years old and in Eugene at the bank, the teller who was waiting on him commented on how beautiful the ring was and asked him how much it had cost. He shrugged his shoulders and told her it was a gift.

As he left the bank, he decided to take it to Goshlin's Jewelers and have the ring appraised. Goshlin's dealt only in exquisite jewelry, and Bobby knew Mr. Goshlin would give him an accurate appraisal.

Bobby had seen Rita Middelton through the store window once when he had driven by, but he was never able to see her clearly. After he found a parking space and turned off the ignition, he lifted his hand and looked at the ring, then he got out of the car, enabling him to get a good look at her. She was always busy behind the counter.

Rita was waiting on a young couple looking at wedding rings. When Bobby entered the store, Rita glanced up at him.

"I'll be right with you, sir." Her smile was enchanting, enhancing her lovely face.

Bobby had always gone for pretty women and thought to himself that he would like to meet her. But he wasn't the kind of man who comes on strong. It was apparent that she was much younger than he was, and he doubted he'd be able to convince himself to reveal his thoughts to her. He knew he couldn't say anything that would make her take a second look at him.

The young couple spent, what seemed to him, half the morning looking at rings. In reality he had only been waiting twenty minutes when he heard the guy ask Rita if he could put the ring they picked out on layaway. That took another five minutes, and Bobby's anxiety grew another inch.

When they finally left, Bobby opened the door for them. The girl was in front.

"Thanks, Gramps," the guy said as he passed in front of Bobby.

Bobby knew he was getting older, although he didn't feel like it, but being called Gramps or Grandpa or even old man was disrespectful, to his way of thinking. He had been raised to address his elders with "sir" and all women with "ma'am," no matter their age.

Rita's eyes were comforting when he spoke, handing his ring to her across the counter. "I'd like to get this appraised, ma'am."

Her slim fingers moved gracefully as she took the ring. Bobby was delighted at seeing no wedding band. *Dang, she has a pretty smile,* he thought, watching her walk down the long glass counter and disappear into a small adjoining room.

In about five minutes Mr. Goshlin came out of the room and walked toward Bobby. Rita was following.

"Hello, Bobby, its been a while. How've you been?" Goshlin greeted when he was across the counter from Bobby. "I suppose the rodeos are keeping you busy," he continued.

Bobby nodded. "We've been busy, all right. My son's running most of the rodeos now. Hank's helping him a lot, but I've slowed down and am taking care of my sheep."

Goshlin held the ring out to Bobby. "This is a very nice diamond. It's worth at least twenty thousand dollars, maybe twenty-five to the right buyer. Are you intending to sell it?"

"No, it was a gift. I've had it a long time and just wanted to know how much it was worth," Bobby said as he took the ring from Goshlin and slipped it on his finger.

The two men visited for a few minutes then shook hands, and Goshlin turned away. Bobby nodded so long to Rita and started to leave.

She spoke. "Are you Bobby Christensen?"

Bobby nodded. "Yes, ma'am."

"I've gone to a lot of your rodeos," Rita said. "I think you put on the best rodeos in the northwest."

Rita's pleasant voice eased his tension and they began a conversation. Her eyes conquered his as each secretly explored the other's persona. It wasn't long before they had dinner together and the seeds of a relationship were planted.

As they ate, Bobby found her fascinating, with everything he liked in a woman. She had class, wasn't foul-mouthed, spoke well, loved horses and rodeos, and was very pretty. Lucille had been the only other woman who had ever stirred butterflies in his stomach until that moment.

Rita found him charming with a gentleness about him that let his strength surface. That was important to her.

We have a lot in common, she thought, noting his good manners as he ate and sipped his coffee quietly. *And even if he is older than I am, so what? His teeth are white, he's not bald, and he's handsome and seems real nice. I wonder if he can dance.*

"Can you dance?" Rita asked.

"You bet. I sure do and I sure like it," Bobby answered.

In his free time, which he didn't have much of, Bobby dated Rita. The most time they could spend together was when he took her to a CB rodeo. They went together for a year before they married.

She was a lot of help at the rodeos, helping with the pickup and flag horses and posting the colors with the girls—Vicki, Sherri, or Kathy.

After the first year of her marriage to Bobby, when he was handling Lewiston and Pendleton (two of the big four, including Salem and Puyallup), Rita drove the tack truck from Lewiston to Pendleton. Kathy had helped Hank and Bobby, Jr. at Salem and drove to Pendleton to help. She had Michelle and Becky with her.

At Pendleton, Rita and Kathy posed the colors for the grand entry. When they charged into the arena the first day, riding two big, good-looking matching sorrels, they were flying.

Kathy slid her horse to a dust-raising stop in her position in front of the grandstand. But one of Rita's bridle reins snapped. The big sorrel was in a dead run. Rita was a good enough hand with a horse that she knew better than to try and stop him with one rein. She let him run past the grandstand and to the fence. Just before he reached it, he stuck his tail in the ground and skidded to a stop.

Everyone in the family loved Rita. She and Bobby had signed on for life, but after nine years the heartbreak of a divorce took over their lives.

35

The Beginning of the End

Way back in 1968, the Christensen Brothers were furnishing the stock at two early September rodeos, Lewiston, Idaho, and Ellensburg, Washington. Bobby needed a few extra horses to use at Ellensburg. He had heard of Harry Vold, but didn't know him or how to locate him.

Harry was living in Asker, Alberta, Canada, where he had lived when he began furnishing bucking horses. He wasn't much more than a kid then and rode bareback horses some. It was in those early years that he decided he'd see if he could put together a little bunch of broncs for a few little amateur rodeos. After he had a little string built up and the contracts for the rodeos, he had to figure out how to get them there. He didn't have a truck and there were no railroad lines to transport the horses, but it wasn't uncommon to drive stock to rodeos at that time. So he and a buddy trailed them.

On one such occasion they had to cross a major river. The water was deep and swift. They knew it would be a "bear-cat" to cross and started discussing the problem, trying to work it out long before they reached the river. As they drew near, they spotted a big barge tied to small dock, rocking lethargically.

When Harry asked the pilot of the barge if he could raft the horses across, the man told him he could float sixty tons across. There would surely be no trouble crossing with seventeen head of horses, counting the two saddle horses.

That was good news, and the two cowboys choused the big feather-legged ponies across the dock. All of them spooked, they balled up on the closest end of the barge, and down she went. The horses all slid into the water and took to swimming. With the weight off, the barge rocked back level, shoveling a big wave of water up on the dock. Harry and his pal spurred their mounts off the dock and onto the barge, and the pilot took them across. They hit a lope, ducking through the brush and trees, until they found the broncs where they had come out of the river.

Years later, when Harry had a pretty fair set of horses and bulls, he turned the outfit over for his son, Wayne, to run. Then he purchased a livestock sale barn and bought and sold cattle, auctioneering the sales himself.

At the Lewiston rodeo, Bobby heard that Wayne Vold had a little amateur rodeo outfit in Canada and called him about leasing some of his stock to use at Ellensburg.

When Wayne talked to his father about it, Harry said they'd send the best broncs they had They helped put on Ellensburg and Pendleton and a couple of more Christensen rodeos. Harry told Bobby he was going to sell his auction barn, buy another bucking string, and go into the rodeo business full-time. He planned to go pro, and let Wayne handle the Canadian rodeos while he handled the ones in the States. And so he did. He bought out Harry Knight after a partnership and was on the road toward a successful journey down the rodeo trail.

On June 14, 1984, Bobby, Jr. told Dave Belyea, a young cowboy about his age who worked on the outfit, that he would haul a load of broncs and two pickup horses back from the rodeo at Livermore, California. There were two loads going, and Dave asked Bobby, Jr. if he could take the truck with the forty best broncs they owned. Dave was a good hand around the ranch and loved the horses. He'd groom the ones that would let him and he was a hard worker. Bobby told him it was the load he had already planned for him to take, and after loading the truck Dave pulled out.

The brakes were a little worn on the truck, but there was no time to repair them. Bobby had called around to different mechanics, but none of them could get to the job before the truck had to roll again.

Dave was no different from any cowboy about his love for music, and the first thing he did after he left Livermore was to turn on the radio. After it had turned dark, Dave turned up the radio to listen closely to a song titled "Someday Soon." Judy Collins had had a hit with it in the seventies. *"Blow you old blue Northern, blow my love to me. He's drivin' in tonight from California. He loves his damned ol' rodeos as much as he loves me . . ."* Those few lines sort of touched Dave as he tapped the steering wheel, keeping time.

The truck was starting down a steep grade and picking up speed.

Dave pushed the brake pedal. There were no brakes! He continued to pump them, but there was nothing. He pulled the trailer brakes. They took hold, but with the heavy load pushing, they began to smoke and soon went out. Dave tried to gear down. He couldn't. The truck was flying.

"Someday soon, goin' with him, someday soon."

There was no pleasure in that line of the song to comfort him. He could only hear the rumbling sound of the vibrating tires on the heavy truckload of horses pulling a load of steers and calves in a bobtail. He saw a guardrail as a long curve shot up in front of him. He managed to make it, and in the distance ahead he could see a see another and sharper curve. The guardrail was on both sides of the highway.

In a panicked state of mind, the only way he could slow the truck down enough to make the upcoming curve was to angle it into the guardrail, and he did. He didn't have the strength to overcome the force of the big front tires against the rail. They climbed it, and the truck shot into the air, dove into the slope of the mountain, flipped, and the doors popped open. Dave flew out of the seat and landed, uninjured. The truck catapulted and turned over in the air two more times before it landed upside-down.

H bar B, Wizz Bang, Smith and Velvet, and Hixon's HighBall were among the fourteen bucking and saddle horses that were killed. Kathy's $5,000 barrel racing horse also lay lifeless, beside the highway. Also on board were thirty roping calves and forty steers, some of which lived.

36

The Fall of the Christensen Empire

It's funny how things happen. One day you can be on top of the world, and the next day you can be faced with the worst day of your life. It happened that way with the Christensen family.

By the early 1980s the outfit was on top, or so everyone thought. They had replaced the horses that were killed in the wreck with forty more. The new ones couldn't compare with the ones they had lost, but they were above average. Their bulls were all healthy and bucking good, and the 5,000 head of ranch cattle and 4,000 head of ewes were all in good shape. The outfit had gotten so big it was hard to realize the impact of their accomplishments.

Every day was filled with hard work of one kind or another, and nobody took a day off. Everyone right down to the kids, old enough to have a driver's license, had a new car.

There was no outside influence on their success, except the many cowboys who had worked for them over the fifty some-odd years they had struggled. The family had run the outfit without the outside help of bookkeepers, business managers, or CPAs.

They had always kept their own books and built up an impeccable line of credit.

As the family gathered in the office inside the main ranch house at the home ranch, little did they know that fate was lying in wait ready to deliver the fatal blow that would bring the empire down.

Henry and Pat, Bobby, Bobby, Jr., Kathy, Linda, Sherri and Rob, Mollie, Bill and Babe Markley and their son Billy, Danny and Vicki, and the ranch's banker from Southern Oregon Production Credit, Arnold Morton, were all present.

Morton threw the first arrow after everyone was settled. He told them they had lost $50,000 that year.

Everyone kind of looked at each other. Hank asked him how that could be possible.

Morton's lips broadened as he answered Hank. "Hell, Hank you could lose that much every year from now on and still never go under. Your land is worth a fortune."

That was nice to hear, but it was a hard bite to swallow. There was no one to blame, but something had gone haywire.

When the meeting broke up and Morton had gone, Hank comforted Mollie with a gentle hand. "I guess we should have taken the seven million we were offered for the outfit years ago."

"Seven and a half million, son," Mollie corrected.

In 1978 they had indeed been offered seven and a half million dollars for the home ranch at Eugene. But Hank figured if they were offering that much then, in ten years they would offer twice that. So they didn't sell.

They had to use their holdings to borrow more money for operating capital. Paying the interest and keeping the outfit going was a big expense, but they were keeping up.

A lot of the bucking horses were beginning to slow down, especially the older ones. There was no doubt they needed to buy new horses if they didn't want to lose their good contracts. And 99 percent of them were good.

Hank and Bobby, Jr. were able to buy some fairly good broncs at a bucking horse sale. They were young enough and about the same caliber as the ones they had bought after losing the great ones in the big truck wreck.

There was a lot of money coming and going, but everything seemed to be making money.

Things went along smoothly until the big bubble burst in 1985, and Southern Oregon Production Credit went under. Being the largest borrower at this bank worried Henry. He was a highly stressed man and had suffered several heart attacks and a stroke.

There were two other Production Credit banks in the money monopoly in lower Oregon besides Southern: Willamette and one more. The banks invested in the fishing business on the Oregon coast and had a stack of loan papers on boats as thick as a telephone book when the first El Niño hit. They had to foreclose on the boat creditors and couldn't peddle the boats elsewhere. They lost $40 million, and along with Southern Oregon Production Credit they went down.

Taking control of the banking disaster was the Federal Land Bank of Spokane. They, too, had suffered losses and were taken over by the Federal Credit Administration. Now called the Farm Credit Bank of Spokane, they foreclosed on the ranches three times but couldn't get them.

The interest on farm loans skyrocketed, and farm families all across America were going under. Willie Nelson was traveling the dusty, country roads giving concerts for Farm Aid.

The Christensens put the Rodeo Company with U.S. Bank in order to operate and buy time to sell the ranches. The Farm Credit Bank was really on the fight now, so Bobby, Jr. filed Chapter 11 and stirred up some buyers. However, the word got around that the outfit was going under, and if and when it did they could buy the whole shebang for fifty cents on the dollar. So the prospective buyers kicked back to wait it out, and the outfit was running out of options.

The Farm Credit Bank was pulling every trick in the book to add the rodeo company's mortgage in with the ranches. They managed to get Bobby, Jr. locked up at the NIRA rodeo at Corvallis and impounded everything: the stock, every pickup horse, every flag horse, every flag, every saddle, the tack trailer loaded with every halter, every flank, and even the stopwatches. They took every solitary thing, except Bobby, Jr.'s spurs and Jesse's pony.

The word was out all over the country that the Farm Credit Bank had the rodeo outfit up for sale.

When someone at U.S. Bank failed to sign a paper correctly, the Farm Credit Bank got the mortgages on the rodeo outfit back.

The days flew by in desperation. Finally, the sheriff's department scheduled a sale at the Benton County fairgrounds to sell the stock. Bobby, Jr. contacted Harry Vold and Bob Thain. They stepped forward without hesitation and bought the rodeo outfit, making an agreement to sell it back to Bobby, Jr. in a year.

The year came and went in no time. Bobby, Jr. was unable to buy the outfit back by himself and began looking for a partner. Tracy Denley was a longtime friend of the family and had always wanted to go into the rodeo business. When Bobby, Jr. approached him with the offer of a partnership, he jumped at it.

Denley put in the biggest share of the money and owned fifty-one percent.

Without the ranches they had to rent pasture for the rodeo stock, and the operating expenses skyrocketed. The outfit folded in 1989, and the remaining assets were sold.

The Christensens began advertising to sell the ranches, but with the word out that they were in a bind, potential buyers were in the lurch waiting for the fall.

Hank wouldn't give up. He got wind of a prospective buyer and contacted the TARA Land and Cattle Company owned by Dan Dingus, first vice president of the First Interstate Bank, and Oliver Hemphill.

Hemphill drove up to the Eugene ranch with a pretty lady at his side in a long, shiny car. After he pushed open his door and got out, he spotted Hank brushing a horse. He walked up to Hank with an outstretched, milky-soft hand, saying he was there to look over the ranch. He told Hank it looked like a nice place.

Little did he know he was about to look at one of the best

ranches in southern Oregon. An outfit built by fifty years of blistering work and the callused hands of a pioneering Oregon family and their descendants.

Hank gave him a tour of the ranch, knowing that these would be his last steps along the old trails they walked.

Hemphill convinced Hank to let him have a lease option to buy the ranch. He said it would take at least five years to pay for it and wasted no time getting the contract drawn up for Hank's signature.

Hemphill made regular trips to the ranch and occasionally took Hank fishing. The others involved in Hank's commitment, Hemphill rudely ignored.

The family had put both ranches together years before, and together they were worth over $10 million. The interest was phenomenal. Hemphill didn't have to pay it; the Christensens did. At 22 percent to Oregon Production Credit, it amounted to $2,000 a day. Making interest payments like that was putting them deeper in the hole daily.

With everyone pitching in, they cut cordwood to sell in order to pay for the electricity and hauled it to the Southern Pacific Railroad.

Whenever Hemphill visited, he always had his briefcase and a story of how he was going to put in an Arabian horse ranch and a vineyard. He was going to cut the oak trees to make his wine barrels. He was getting the money together—or was he? The Christensens believed he was. But it didn't happen. Only God and Hemphill know why he tied the outfit up for five years, but he did and pulled out.

The family more than likely would have sold it to someone else long before the five years were up, but the five-year deal kept them bound.

Now the outfit was desperate. Hank and Bobby tried everyone they could think of. Finally, Bobby, Jr., contacted Virgil Howard, a distant cousin of Danny Tatum. He wasted no time in coming to the rescue. Howard, a developer in Danville, California, had heard the Christensens were in trouble and flew up to give Bobby $8,000 to help him file bankruptcy. He would buy the ranches and sign the papers in federal court to make the payments. But fate's shadow grew longer when Howard defaulted on a payment. He was the Christensens' last hope.

The Farm Credit Bank got it all back. They auctioned both the Eugene and Happy Valley ranches off on the steps of the courthouse. A German bought the home place. He was a square shooter who paid $500,000 in cash for it. (He has since died, and his wife owns it now.)

A few gloomy, hushed moments hung on the kitchen walls in the main house at the Eugene ranch. All the family was there as Mollie spoke. Her old eyes held the deep humbleness of the Bohemian pioneer foundation she had passed down to her children, grandchildren, and great-grandchildren.

There was strength in her words as her eyes drifted over the family. "We started with nothing, so we've lost nothing."

Mollie moved to Corvallis to live with Babe until she passed away at the ripe old age of ninety-nine. Hank and Pat stayed on the Eugene ranch for a short time before they told the homeplace a teary goodbye.

A man out of California was waiting in the wings with a suitcase full of money to buy the Happy Valley Ranch and did.

It was a dreary time as everyone drove away, leaving memories and Bobby, Sr. behind. Bobby, Sr. had been told he could stay on the place in the little house he had shared with Lucille many years before.

Things that might be trivial to some were tough on Bobby, and the little cowboy only stayed a short while before pulling out.

Over their prospering years, the Christensens had paid $90,000 a year in interest to the Federal Land Bank on loans, plus $250,000 a year on an operating loan and over $900,000 to Oregon Production Credit Associations. Adding those amounts with the taxes they paid for all those years, then throwing in sixty years of blood, sweat, tears and heartache, *and ending up with nothing,* is a dirty rotten shame, to say the least.

Hank grieved over the loss for six months before he passed away. His life was really over when everything began to fall apart. He loved the outfit; it was as much a part of him as his arms. The land, the saddle horses, the rodeo string, the farming, the cattle and sheep. The little lambs he babied as though they were his flesh and blood.

One stormy winter day, long before the crisis hit, there were some baby lambs hung up in the mud. He pulled the fenders off his brand new Cadillac, put mud tires on, and hauled the lambs out of the bog in the trunk of the car. He loved animals.

Harry Vold was at Hank's side one day in the hospital. It must have been tough for Harry to hear Hank's weak voice.

"Now, promise me you'll get some new broncs, Harry," Hank would say. "And get good ones. We always had the best."

The doctor said his death was caused by a heart attack. But many think he died from heartbreak.

Epilogue
by Billy Wilcoxson

It would take a book twice the size of this one to list all the friends who have come and gone since Lawrence and Mollie Christensen became one. There were no black marks in the family's past, nor are there any in the present.

I've grown to love this family over the few months it has taken me to write this story. They have shown me the respect, kindness, and warmth any man could want; the qualities their heavenly ancestors bequeathed to them.

They were hard-working, persistent country folks, generous to a fault. And they remain so. After the outfit broke up, family members walked away, stunned. What had been a way of life for generations suddenly existed no more.

It was a difficult time for them all, to say the least. What trails to take with no direction to follow?

Marriages began to stumble and soon fell by the wayside. A family once so very close had torn apart at the seams, each of them coping differently with their emotions of pain and memories, both good and bad.

While writing this book and interviewing many of the family members, it was plain to see that some still hurt deep inside their hearts. But they show strength without harboring any bitterness.

It was once written that "When the going gets tough, the tough get going." And that is exactly what the Christensen family has done.

Albert Bobby Christensen can be proud. After all, it is not what we accumulate in our way along life's mysterious paths, but rather the treasures we can offer life and what love we can sprinkle along the way.

The Christensen name is still heard above the applause of the audience and still spoken behind the chutes. Not only by the old-timers who remember, but also by a whole new generation of cowboys.

Bobby's grandsons, Brett Tatum and Jesse Christensen, are both top-notch Christian cowboys and PRCA members. Brett rides bulls, and Jesse rides bareback horses. Neither chose rodeo; rodeo chose them. Jesse and wife Addie reside in Odessa, Texas; Brett and wife Keylie live in Wickenburg, Arizona.

Sherri Christensen is living in Loraine, Oregon, raising her two daughters, Josie Dee and Sammy Jo.

Linda Christensen is married to Mel Parkhurst and living in Onalaska, Washington. Linda's two daughters, Amy and Anna, live and work in Seattle. Bobby, Jr. and wife Nancy live and work out of Arlington, Oregon. Kathy Christensen lives in Phoenix, Arizona. Kathy and Bobby Jr.'s two daughters, Michelle and Becky, live in Spokane, Washington.

Peggy Christensen, Henry's oldest daughter, died of a heart attack in 1996.

Bill Markley is deceased, as well as his son, Bill, Jr. (Billy).

Martha "Babe" Markley is eighty-six and still has the Christensen spice. She lives with her youngest son, Gary, and his family in Corvallis, Oregon.

Vickie Christensen Felder and her husband, Eddie, live in Bloomfield, New Mexico.

Albert Bobby Christensen, ninety years young, and as healthy as a bull calf, is happy and content living near his daughter and her family in New Mexico. He still makes a trip each fall to the place where "his heart will always be," in Oregon, to buy feeder lambs and hunt elk with his friends Max Elder and Larry Jackson.

The legacy of the Christensen family will live as long as there are horses that buck and cowboys to ride them.

Glossary

bares: bareback broncs (cowboy slang)
bench-legged: short
black bottom: type of dance popular in the Roaring Twenties
boar: male bear
bobtail: type of truck not pulling a trailer
brad against the back of chute: a horse mashing rider in chute (cowboy slang)
broke in two, breaks in two: when a horse begins bucking (cowboy slang)
browme: lower gear in truck transfer case
bulldog "bulldog a steer": steer wrestling, throwing a steer by hand
catch colt: breeding from unknown sire (cowboy slang)
cayuse: tough little horse
choppo: Mexican for blocky built (cowboy slang)
chouse: yell at or chase cattle
cribbing: scaffolding
curb kickers, "Tony Lama curb kickers": cowboy boots made by Tony Lama (cowboy slang)
daily: to wrap or turn rope around saddlehorn
diamond hitch: used to secure loads on pack animals
dinked: tired
earmark: notch cut in the ears of cattle to identify
friction sticks: levers that cause friction on brakes to turn bulldozer
Hamley: make of bronc saddle

hondo: small loop in the end of a lariat rope
hoot: roundup-cook's helper (cowboy slang)
in the well: down on rider's riding hand side of a spinning bull (cowboy slang)
morrales: homemade feedbags made of burlap
mustang: Indian pony
mutton-withered, flat-withered: very low withers
oiled up: drunk (cowboy slang)
oxbows: type of narrow stirrup used to ride broncs
ox crotchers: bull riders
panniers: canvas bags used for supplies that hang on sawbuck
perf: performance (cowboy slang)
pick up: ride a horse next to a bucking horse to get rider off
pickupman: man responsible for getting rider off a bucking horse
pooped off: bucked off
prairie schooner: a large covered wagon
rank: bucking animal that is difficult to ride
remuda: string or herd of horses
sawbucks: wooden saddles used on pack animals
seven under bit: a 7 notch cut in the bottom of the ears of cattle
soggy, "big soggy": big, well-built horse (cowboy slang)
swallow fork: a V notch in the ears of cattle
tapped off: getting in time with bucking horse (cowboy slang)
tooter: eight-second whistle signaling end of ride (cowboy slang)
trace chains: chains that connect the team's harness to a wagon
turning the crank: an animal that is bucking hard (cowboy slang)
***vultas*, California style:** *vultas*—Mexican for daily; California style—fast (cowboy slang)
wheelers: team closest to the wagon
whip, "whips in the herd": bucking animal easy to ride; "whip cream" (cowboy slang)
"who shot John": whiskey, or being "whiskied up" (cowboy slang)
withers: bony protuberance at the base of a horse's neck

Appendix

I. CHRISTENSEN BROTHERS NFR STOCK

1961
BAREBACKS
Three Corners
Mighty Mouse
Smokey
Red Devil
Strawberry Shake

SADDLE BRONCS
Desert Rat
Bimbo
No Dice
Ace of Spades
Try Me
Brown Bomber

BULLS
Snowman
Sleepy
Droopy
High Noon

1962
BAREBACKS
Woodburn
Burnt River

SADDLE BRONCS
Gutherie Dun
Desert Rat
Bimbo

BULLS
Big Ed
High Noon
Geronimo
Droopy
Snowman

1963
BAREBACKS
Brown Tee
Smitty—2nd NFR
High Society

War Dance
Mighty Mouse

SADDLE BRONCS
Jet Liner
Woodburn
Desert Rat
Hart Mountain
Stringeree

BULLS
Snowman
Geronimo
High Noon
Big Ed
Trouble Shooter—3rd NFR

1964
BAREBACKS
Smitty
High Society
Teacher's Pet
Red Devil
Simple Simon
Burnt River

SADDLE BRONCS
Rocky Rail
Desert Rat
Copper Mountain
Woodburn

BULLS
Trouble Shooter
Snuffy

Iceman
Missoula

1965
BAREBACKS
High Society
Quick Change—2nd NFR

SADDLE BRONCS
Double O
Smitty
Quick Silver

BULLS
Snuffy
Trouble Shooter
Missoula

1966
BAREBACKS
High Society—2nd NFR
Party Doll

SADDLE BRONCS
Smitty
Blue Rocket

BULLS
Tommy
Missoula
Snuffy
Mr. Johnson
Wilfred—Best Bull/Year

1967
BAREBACKS
High Society
Party Doll
Quick Change

SADDLE BRONCS
Smitty
Desert Rat
Drifter

BULLS
Wilfred
Snuffy
Missoula—Best Bull/Year

1968
BAREBACKS
Party Doll
Quick Change
Burnt River
Mr. Smith

SADDLE BRONCS
Drifter
Smitty
Quimosabe
Copper Mountain
Warrior Creek

BULLS
Snuffy
Wilfred—2nd NFR
Missoula
Tommy

1969
BAREBACKS
Party Doll
Burnt River
Big Al
Quick Change
Billy Buck

SADDLE BRONCS
Smitty
Drifter
Quimosabe

BULLS
Missoula
Wilfred
Snuffy
Tommy
White Hope

1970
BAREBACKS
Party Doll
Burnt River
Bimbo
Big Al
Legs
Country Cousin

SADDLE BRONCS
Smitty
Drifter
Checkmate
Shenandoah

BULLS
Missoula
Wilfred
Snuffy
Tommy
White Hope

1971
BAREBACKS
Party Doll
Burnt River
Bimbo
Jack of Diamonds
Brown Tee

SADDLE BRONCS
Smitty
Checkmate
Shenandoah
Quick Silver

BULLS
Wilfred
Tommy
White Hope

1972
BAREBACKS
Smitty
Party Doll
Jack of Diamonds
Little John

SADDLE BRONCS
Checkmate
Quick Silver
Night Train

BULLS
Wilfred
Nitro

1973
BAREBACKS
Party Doll
Jack of Diamonds
Misfit

SADDLE BRONCS
Checkmate
Quick Silver
Shenandoah
Smitty
Fallout
Hot Line

BULLS
Wilfred
Geronimo
Rapid Fire
WhirlAway

1974
BAREBACKS
Party Doll
Jack of Diamonds
Wine Glass

SADDLE BRONCS
Check Mate—Buck Horse/Yr
Smitty
Quick Silver
Felix
Shenandoah

BULLS
Wilfred
Geronimo

1975
BAREBACKS
Capone
Tea Party
Mr. Smith—didn't send

SADDLE BRONCS
Checkmate
Smitty
Quick Silver

BULLS
None

1976
BAREBACKS
Mr. Smith
Party Doll

SADDLE BRONCS
Big John
Checkmate
Smitty
Jeremiah

BULLS
Snuffy
Play Mate
Wolf Guard
Mtn Maw

1977
BAREBACKS
Mr. Smith—BB/year

SADDLE BRONCS
Big Jack
Checkmate
Smitty
Brown Tee
Jeremiah—2nd NFR

BULLS
Big Red
Ground Split
Snuffy
Play Mate
Floyd Cook

1978
BAREBACKS
Mr. Smith
Little John
ZX
Golden Glow

SADDLE BRONCS
Big Jake
Checkmate
Jeremiah
June's Pride

BULLS
Big Red
Play Mate
Ground Split
Snuffy
Sox

1979
BAREBACKS
Smith and Velvet
Party Doll
Sassy Sue
Bo Jangles
Little John

SADDLE BRONCS
National Velvet
Grey Eagle
Henry Special
Brown Tea

BULLS
Ground Split
Soxs
Angus

1980
BAREBACKS

Smith and Velvet BB/Year
Dandy Dan
Red Lady

SADDLE BRONCS
National Velvet
Henry Special
Grey Eagle
H-B

BULLS
Velvet Playmate
Flintstone

1981
BAREBACKS
Smith and Velvet
Check Mate
Red Lady
Rusty
Fancy Velvet

SADDLE BRONCS
National Velvet
H-B
Hixon High Ball

BULLS
Oscar's Velvet
Flints Velvet

1982
BAREBACKS
Smith and Velvet—BB/Year

Fancy
Spider
Red Lady

SADDLE BRONCS
National Velvet
H-B

BULLS
Oscar's Velvet—3rd NFR
Paleface

1983
BAREBACKS
Sitting Bull
National Velvet
Red Devil

SADDLE BRONCS
Whiz Bang
Northwestern

BULLS
Oscar's Velvet—BB/Year
Paleface

1984
BAREBACKS
John Wayne
Red Devil

SADDLE BRONCS
Whiz Bang
Rusty

BULLS
Oscar's Velvet
Paleface

1985
BAREBACKS
John Wayne
Western Express
Ellie Lewis

SADDLE BRONCS
Northwestern

BULLS
Oscar's Velvet
Paleface

II. Famous Christensen Brothers Saddle Broncs

MISS KLAMATH: A sensational bucking horse that was purchased in 1951 from the Klamath Indians, Klamath Falls, Oregon. Miss Klamath had a near perfect score in the arena; she was successfully ridden only once. She had bucked off many famous saddle bronc riders: Deb Copenhaver, Billy Weeks, Casey Tibbs, Sonny Fureman, and many others.

SATAN SISTER: A small pinto mare that tested the bronc rider every time she jumped into the arena. She came from eastern Oregon (more good bucking horses were found more often in eastern Oregon than any other parts of the United States). She was very gentle in every way but her bucking ability.

TRY ME: One of the all-time great bucking horses of the Christensen Brothers string. A chunky bay horse that took many a cowboy to the pay window, just as many have failed on Try Me.

RED RIVER: A once gentle saddle horse that found his way to the bucking string from Sonora, California. The sorrel horse could be counted on to spin right out of the chute. Red River was difficult to pick-up because spinning all the time he could easily injure pickupmen and horse with his wild kicking.

HAPPY LANDING: A bay horse that weighed over 1,400 pounds and made the longest jump from the chute of any horse in the string. Could always be counted on to jump right straight into the air out of the chute. One to watch—Happy Landing.

BIG ENUFF: A big black horse that for over three years was placed on every time he was ridden. He commanded the respect of every saddle bronc rider who ever tried to ride him. He was one of the many Canadian horses in the Christensen Brothers string.

SKID ROW SUE: A small pinto mare that came from a riding school in Seattle, Washington. Purchased by the Christensen Brothers at the Western Washington Fair, Puyallup, Washington, in 1949.

CROWFOOT: A big black horse that would fight all the time, even when being fed or led to water. He was nervous in the chute and wanted to hit the arena in a hurry.

Snafu, One Spot, Bald Hornet, Brief Moments, Detour, May Day, Challenger, and Black Powder were all top saddle broncs.

III. Famous Christensen Brothers Bulls

LEFTY: This bull was raised by the Christensen Brothers and had been bucked for six years, being ridden only nine times. He was a small spotted bull that would spin and had a remarkable record to his credit.

BULL DURHAM: A brindle bull that looked just like the bull in the Bull Durham cigarette ads. He was perhaps the most gentle bull in the rodeo string. After bucking off his rider, he just walked off and looked for the way out.

GOLDEN GRAIN: This bull was raised on a bottle after his mother died. He liked to be petted but would get mean in the chute and would buck the boys off, then try to hurt them.

LITTLE BOYCE: A bull that had to be tied in the chute so a bull rider could get on. He would fight.

Henry Lawrence Christensen
(1911–1986)

An empty saddle in the arena today, Henry Christensen passed away.

Widely known for his horses and bulls and his know-how for getting the grandstands full.

War Paint and Miss Klamath were just a few, High Society and Northwestern and Mighty Mouse, too!

Hank was a man we all loved dear, and I wish today he could be here. But when the Lord called, Hank had to go.

For the Lord wanted him to put on a good rodeo.

Louie Zabala

BILLY WILCOXSON grew up on a ranch in New Mexico. The Navy veteran attended college in California and Arizona before becoming a rodeo cowboy and Hollywood stuntman. He is the author of a book, *Ten Karat Hole in a Donut,* a screenplay, *The Legend of Pearl Hart and Joe Boot,* and is a songwriter as well.

www.ingramcontent.com/pod-product-compliance
Lightning Source LLC
Chambersburg PA
CBHW020751160426
43192CB00006B/304